ZICO: AN AUTOBIOGRAPHY OF A NON-LEAGUE FOOTBALLER

Ryan-Zico Black

authorHOUSE®

AuthorHouse™ UK Ltd.
500 Avebury Boulevard
Central Milton Keynes, MK9 2BE
www.authorhouse.co.uk
Phone: 08001974150

First published by AuthorHouse 4/17/2008

ISBN: 978-1-4343-5341-2 (sc)

Printed in the United States of America
Bloomington, Indiana

This book is printed on acid-free paper.

ACKNOWLEDGEMENTS

I would like to give a big thanks to my mum and dad who have always given me there full support and helped me which ever way they can. If they hadn't been so supportive when I was younger I wouldn't have had the experiences I've been able to have.

My sister Dionne– Maire who had to put up with non-stop football at both Rio de Janeiro and San Siro Milan our two houses when we were kids.

I would like to thank Becky my girlfriend who is always there for me and has had to listen to my moaning when I've not been playing well. Which is probably been a fair bit. And everything else that comes with being with a footballer like New Years Eve staying in and Friday nights. The front cover which Becky designed I'm also very proud of.

To all my team mates I have played with through out my career it's been a pleasure and I've shared some good and bad times with many.

Thanks to Steve Rodrigues who had read an article about the book in the Lancashire Evening Post and then contacted me to say he would help as much as he could which I think was great of him.

To the rest of my family and friends outside of football in Guernsey, Lancashire and elsewhere.

I hope you all enjoy the book.

Chapter 1

Born In Guernsey

FROM THE MOMENT I could I was kicking a football. My mum still has the first ball that I was kicking lying flat on my back with a small soft ball on a piece of string.

It was to be that my Irish father Dessie Black, a big fan of Celtic and the great Brazil decided to christen me Zico but as my mum saw to it I was named Ryan-Zico Black, she was worried that I might not like football so a compromise was met. When growing up I always spelled my name with a line through the z after I got Ossie Ardiles autograph when he was playing for Spurs against Guernsey, I was mascot for Guernsey that day.

Years ago Guernsey hosted a number of top class sides from England with all the big names coming over and the local players getting a chance to play against some of the best players around. Unfortunately there haven't been any teams over for a few years Everton being one of the last teams.

I was born in Guernsey on the 4th of August 1981 to my mother Sue Black and father Dessie. Both of my parents have always been sporty, I remember watching my dad playing football on a Saturday for local side Bells and then on a Sunday it would be Tiger City or Doyle Road plus midweek 5 a side. I used to dread watching them Sunday games sometimes, there was always one of his team mates if not himself getting sent off. Most of the team at Tiger were Irish, Scottish and English with one or two locals. They are funny memories though and I was always kicking a ball around or watching dad play. I was in the same team as him once on a Sunday when I was about 16 he was buzzing saying how great it is to playing on the same team as my son, he was sent off after 5 minutes. His team was full of characters though and they were all mates, the social side of things was definitely as important as the football and was a good excuse for them all to get out on the drink. Dad was a good footballer skilful and scored for fun at the levels he was playing.

Dad had played at a good level of football growing up in Northern Ireland he played for a team called The Star of the Sea. A famous team mainly because they were one of the first mixed teams in Ireland with both Catholic and protestant players in the side. Bobby Sands, the Irish political prisoner who died whilst on a hunger strike was also in the team along with my dad's best friend Willy Caldwell. I remember dad being on panorama when they did a special feature on the star of the sea team and Bobby Sands who became world famous during his time in prison. Since then Sir Andrew Lloyd Webber has made a musical of the Star of the Sea team, it is called The Beautiful Game. They were one of the best teams about at their time in Ireland in their age group. He also played for Fareham and Eastleigh non-league teams in Southampton. Dad was playing there whilst my mum was studying to be a nurse there. He enjoyed it there playing at a decent level but as mum was finishing her studying and was expecting me they went back home to Guernsey. My mum passed her nursing training and became what she always wanted to be a nurse, and a very good one. She had done all sorts of nursing, nights and days as a staff nurse and is now a Specialist nurse at a specialist medical group in Guernsey along with doctors who specialise in specific illnesses. Dionne-Maire my sister was born 3 years and 1 day after me on the 5th of August 1984. Dees is also very sporty although growing up at our house was very much football. She was into all sports netball, hockey, and excelled in swimming.

My first game that I can remember was when my dad was manager of Bells under 13s; I was 8 years old. I had played games younger but this one I remember well, my dad substituted me in the second half and I was fuming mad. I stormed off the pitch and swore at dad, went into the car and slammed the door. I was small to be playing really but I was pestering him for a game and they were short so he gave in. Some of the players who played against me that day still bring it up if I see them out even now in Guernsey. I was a mini at Bells when I played for Guernsey under 11s against Jersey in Jersey it was a massive game for me at the time. We won 4-2 and I scored 2, the game was videoed by one of the boy's father John Stead his son was called John also. A big man with a strong Yorkshire accent and a lovely guy who was always at his sons games. Young John played for Rovers and North and was a good player at youth level unfortunately his father past away a few years ago.

Notre Dame de Rosaire Primary school was my first school. A very good academic school, and a Roman Catholic school run by a nun who was head teacher her name was Sister Marie Paul. I wasn't really interested in schoolwork from day one but had 2 good sports teachers who were nice they were called Mr Darling and Mrs Maclure. I played in a 6 a side tournament up at Haute Capelles school once which they have every year, we got to the semi finals which wasn't bad because only another lad and me played football regularly. Our goalkeeper and my best friend during primary and secondary Martin Yabsley was massive even then. He is 6 foot 9 now and a professional basketball player but he was one useless goalkeeper but was big so we stuck him in there and he got in the way of most shots that came his way.

When I was 11 I had a trial at Southampton. I played a game for them and done well although I was a bit younger than the rest. I continued to go over to Southampton to play and train for a further 3 years and enjoyed it immensely. It was great going to see the first team playing and Matt Le Tissier who was a hero when I was growing up and I still have great admiration for him now for what he produced on the pitch, class. My dad had coached him for a while when he was younger playing at local side Vale Rec. I was flying back and forth to Southampton up until I was 14 and I would go for about 2 weeks at a time. I went for 6 weeks one summer, which was a bit tough being away from my family. My parents obviously missed me but they knew it would be good for my football and I was prepared for the sacrifice. I knew it was what I always wanted to be doing, playing football at the best level I could. It was tough playing against better kids than I was used to in Guernsey and everyone else seemed to be so big and strong compared to me. Southampton had sorted digs out for me and I was staying with a couple called Bill and Wendy who lived in a sky scraper in a flat near the top, in Southampton. Wendy was a sister of a scout who was working for Southampton FC his name was Tony Challis, what a character he was. It was funny the first time I met him I was with my mum and dad and another lad called Will Benfield from Alderney who was on trial. Mum had spoken to him a few times on the phone and said he had sounded very professional and sounded quiet posh. So it was a shock when we all walked off the plane to see are names being held up on card by Tony in his trademark tracksuit courtesy of Southampton, we would find out he didn't take it off. Tony had really long shabby hair, wearing a really long saints jacket and was unshaven, he was a great guy though and ive fond memories of the man. My dad had known Chris Nicholl who was manager at the time and he got a few other Guernsey lads a trial. They used to stay at Tony's, he used to get a few quid for it which was supposed to be for the lads food but they said there was never much food in so they were always getting take away food.

The youth coach was Stuart Henderson, his coaching sessions were good, it was at the Dell indoors in the gym. I loved it at Southampton and was doing really well holding my own with the other lads. I should have stayed there really but Tony had a falling out with saints and left to join Bournemouth so I went there and signed schoolboy forms.

CHAPTER 2

SIGNING SCHOOLBOY FORMS

I WAS PROUD AS punch at the time thinking I had made it, far from it, as I would find out later on. My first year there was great and I was doing well, Bournemouth paid for my flights over in the school holidays and paid my digs too. I played in a tournament in the Isle of Wight against some local teams there I scored a hat trick in one game and had played well in training and in matches. Everything was going to plan. My dad and Tony Challis had got some Guernsey lads over for trials, it was good having a few people there that I knew for a week. All good lads they were Justin le Tissier, Matts cousin, David Rosamond, Malcolm Symons, Neil Sarahs, Chris Chamberlain, Craig Tyrell. None of the lads got taken on but 2 got offered deals. Scott Bradford who has always been a close friend for years went to Preston for 2 years before coming back to Guernsey a few years after. He could be play Scotty but suffered a couple of nasty injuries and Chris Tardif who went to Portsmouth. Chris is at Oxford now after playing league games for Pompey and then Bournemouth on loan. Both good players I played with both of them at local Guernsey team Vale Rec. I hadn't seen Chris for years since we were younger and it was funny when I got called up for the Northern Ireland under 21 squad to play Malta over in Malta. I arrived at the airport to see Chris there. It was a good trip we were both on the bench and had a couple of beers after the game in the hotel. Not sure where his Irish roots were though, he did tell me I think but I can't remember.

Here is my sob story at Bournemouth! It's a true one though. When the time came for them to decide whether or not to take me on as a YTS, I had just broken my arm in a Priaulx league game for Rec away against Rovers in Guernsey. I went for a diving header that I was nowhere near and landed on my arm. I was just 15 nearly 16. I went over to Bournemouth for two weeks my last chance to impress, it was 3 weeks after my injury and I wasn't fit, with that I got an ear infection the day before I went and couldn't hear a word the coach Sean ODriscoll was saying. Sean went on to manage the first team and is now manager at Doncaster. He is softly spoken he was then anyway. I struggled like mad for two weeks and was well off the pace and trying to cover up that I was ill. I played two under 18 games for them and didn't do the best. At the end of the two weeks I even said to him that I should have waited to come over when I was fit. It didn't make much difference; I received a letter from the club saying that due to the club going into receivership they can only take on local based players. I was gutted and couldn't help but think I had blown my chances by rushing over there, but it wasn't to be and that's that, it certainly wouldn't be the last knock back I got from a football club.

Lots of players go through things like that all the time, being released by a club and being told your not good enough, not what we are looking for, surplus to requirements, transfer listed, and that's the nicer ones. Footballers, who have been at Premier League clubs from the age of 12 or younger to 20 and then get released, you'd think they would definitely get a pro club in the league. It doesn't always work like that and I have met lots of players who have nose dived through the leagues and struggled to get a game at conference level and below.

In non-league football a lot of players are signed on non-contract forms, where you sign the normal forms of register, but you don't sign a contract. The benefit of this for the player is that most of the time you will get cash in hand. Another is if you are doing well any club can put a 7 days notice to your club for you that they wish to sign you, and after them 7 days you can speak to that club, so clubs are not put off by transfer fees etc.

The down side of a non-contract which I found out first hand while I was at Northwich Victoria. I was rushed to sign by the manager Steve Davis who wanted to get me signed for the Saturday game away at Halifax so I signed a non contract. Two weeks later he was sacked and a new manager Alvin Macdonald came to the club, when he arrived he obviously wanted to bring his own players in so the first thing he did was to get rid of the non-contract players. I actually played about 10 games for Alvin and was the last player to leave who was on non-contract but he couldn't get rid of contract players even on loan, that's the players right to if they don't wish too, I was released and without a club. Even in the league players are signed on a week to week basis or a month to month. Its not as stable as a contract where you know you are going to get paid every week for the season but in non league a lot of players prefer not to be tied down.

After hearing the bad news at Bournemouth I was now playing at Vale Rec my local team, I made my debut for their first team at 15. In Guernsey there are 7 clubs and each club has 3 teams, the leagues are called the Priaulx, Jackson and Railway league. All football is amateur over there, the biggest games of the year at club level are against Jersey teams in the Upton. Which is a game between the winner of the Guernsey league versus the winner of the Jersey league. The Murrati Vase Trophy is Guernsey versus. Jersey, the game takes place once a year. Alderney are in this competition as well and Guernsey and Jersey take turns each to play Alderney in the semi finals, which Alderney rarely get a win. The Murrati Vase Trophy normally attracts a big crowd but has probably decreased through the years, as has the standard of island football so people say over there.

The youth football in Guernsey produces some talented kids. The problem over there for young players I think is when reaching a certain age they come to a stand still. Being on an island you don't face any stronger or competitive competition therefore players lose interest or are happy in a comfort zone and don't really get any better. So if a kid wants to become a professional footballer from Guernsey he needs to move over to England at 16 or get into an academy at an early age where he can go over in school holidays and play and train with better coaching and better players. It isn't all that easy to become a professional footballer coming from Guernsey for the fact of that stretch of water, separating the island from mainland England is some what of a barrier. Scouts from clubs in England rarely if ever visit Guernsey to look at players so it is down to the individual and possibly there local football club to help in finding a club or going on trials. It is also difficult leaving the comfortable and laid back lifestyle of Guernsey with all of its security's and it is of no surprise that a person would take the safer option of staying there. But for me there was only one job that I wanted to do and I was determined to live out my dream.

There have been several players who have left Guernsey to pursue a career in the game. The most successful player to come from Guernsey is Matt Le Tissier who played for Southampton and went on to play for England. Lee Luscombe also had a spell with Southampton and Leyton Orient. David Waterman who played a lot of games for Portsmouth and went on play for Oxford in the league and moved into non-league with Weymouth and is now at Fareham I think, his brother Lee was a YTS at Portsmouth. Also a YTS at Portsmouth was Michel Wilson who is now back on the island playing along with Ryan Tippet, Kevin Gilligan, Scott Bradford, Grant Chalmers, Tony Vance who all had short spells with Tranmere Rovers, Celtic, Preston North end, Leyton Orient, Wycombe Wanderers respectively. My cousin Darren Martin was also a schoolboy at Bristol City before getting released. Jersey has had 4 or 5 players who have gone over to England for spells in the game. One player who I can think of that's still playing in non-league is Mark Whiteman who signed for Manchester United before going to Bury and dropping in to non-league with Weymouth, Lewes, Havant and WaterlooVille among others. A couple of players in Jersey have done YTS for teams like Celtic and Leeds and again gone home after being released. Another Guernsey player Craig

Allan went in another direction with his football which turned out to be a great move for him, he went to America where he had a very successful career playing a lot of his professional football in the indoor leagues there. A lot of players have gone away to England through the years on trials and short term contracts only to return to the island with homesickness and it is easy to see why Guernsey has a very strong hold on you and its not that easy to leave. When I'm visiting home I am happy that I am going to be leaving again to be playing football. I was playing in the under 18s and first team at Vale Rec, also whilst I was at Bournemouth I was representing Guernsey at under 15s 16s and 18s. I remember a good game for the under 15 Star Trophy side versus Jersey. We won 3-0 and I scored a hat trick. After the game a Leeds scout approached me saying he wanted me to go up there for a trial. I was signed at Bournemouth at the time and asked them for permission to go, but they refused. After my release from Bournemouth it was back to square one and I wasn't sure what to do next. I was back playing for Rec and enjoying it but I knew I wanted to get away.

In the summer with the Vale Rec senior squad we went to France for an annual fixture against a French side. It was a great trip and I enjoyed the game too. We played the French clubs second team and done ok. Our manager was Chris Hamon at the time, Chris and I had a long chat about what I was going to do about my football. Chris suggested the possibility of me staying in France, near the end of the trip I nearly stayed to go and train with the local team there who were a semi-professional outfit but didn't in the end. The place where we were in the south was a small village in the middle of nowhere. I was the youngest there on the trip and I remember picking up the wrong bag at the airport and not finding out until we got to our destination where we were staying after about 10 hours on a bus. I had to borrow some of the lad's clothes for the week taking turns who to borrow off of, there was some bad gear amongst them.

When I got back to Guernsey I was offered a trial at Plymouth Argyle. I spoke with them and they seemed really keen so I did a lot of training before I got there and was looking forward to it. Unfortunately in the second lap of the track on the first day of training I badly sprained my ankle ligaments, it was painful but

I was more disappointed with the fact I couldn't train. Norman Medhurst was the physiotherapist at Plymouth, he was the England physiotherapist when Graham Taylor was the manager and a really nice guy. He treated me for 6 weeks every day but I was still not right and when I tried to join in training it went again. I got the plane back to Guernsey there wasn't any point in hanging around injured, not before a night out in Plymouth with one of the professionals there.

A Geordie who was on trial called Graham Anthony. It was a good night out and I remember putting on a Geordie accent for the night, I was 16. When I recovered from injury I was back at Vale Rec. I was the youngest in the team and it was a good crack, the lads were taking me out into town all the time at weekends and getting me into pubs and on bus party's where you get taken around several pubs all over the island by bus. It was all great fun with a great bunch of lads but I still new I needed to get away to England.

I wrote to lots of clubs in the south of England sending my c.v. And asking for a trial, my parents were very supportive and they said that if I got a trial somewhere they would help with my flights. I received a few letters back from clubs, it was getting late in the day for clubs taking on YTS and most clubs had filled there quotas. Reading was a club who had wrote back offering me a trial so my family and I flew over and I trained 2 days with them and played a game against Bournemouth at there place my old club the reading youth coach was Steve Keen who later became assistant manager at Fulham. I had a great game and things couldn't have gone better in the match. Steve said he was impressed and it was out of me and another lad who was being released by Leeds, he was their first choice but he had a few options and if he didn't accept a deal they would sign me. He did accept and I was a bit down hearted after this knock back as I had played well and felt I was better than what they had, but it is the coaches choice. We weren't a wealthy family despite a lot of people who don't live on Guernsey have the misconception of everyone on Guernsey is rich, not the case unfortunately for us.

CHAPTER 3

A BET WITH A TEACHER AND A JOB!

I HAD FINISHED MY GCSE exams at St Peter Port school where my attendance record wasn't fantastic, and near the end of my schooling I was turning up mainly for P.E and football or Basketball matches so I was surprised when I actually passed a few exams. The P.E teacher was a Welshman called Mr Davies, he was a good teacher who tried to get me to attend the theory lessons with little affect but new I would do well for him in the football and basketball teams. I remember my geography teacher well and I liked her although she was strict and could get wound up with my lack of enthusiasm. She annoyed me one time though, she was frustrated with me for some reason so said to me that I should think of other jobs besides football and I wont be seeing you play on TV ever, I bet her 20 pound I would. I did manage to play a couple of games in a televised conference match and on Match of The day when I was at Morecambe we reached the FA Cup 3rd round against Ipswich Town who were 3rd in the Premiership at the time mid way through the season. I saw her out at a restaurant a year after, I gave her a bit of stick about the bet. Teachers should be more supportive to kids who are wanting to do something that maybe doesn't fit into the normal ideas that are drummed into you when you are young of what you should become when you are older, she agreed and we had a laugh about it. I could see what she was trying to get across to me that it is important to have other interests and a back up in case your dream doesn't materialise but at the same time dreams should be encouraged. I didn't get that 20 pound but settled for a beer.

In Guernsey I needed to earn some money so I got a job with my dads friend who was a carpenter Dave McGall, a big Irishman who could play a bit in his day I was told. I was his apprentice for 2 weeks but then quit after I waited for payday on the Friday after doing a week in hand. I was expecting a couple of hundred pound only to open the envelope of 30 pounds. I was devastated my dad was there and he was holding back a smile after he saw my face. I wasn't the best at it anyway so it was probably a good thing. A couple of weeks later I had a letter through the post from Exeter City inviting me for a trial. I was ready to get on the plane again; it was a trial match, when I arrived for the game there was another Guernsey lad who was a goalkeeper Joel de Wolfsan. I had played well in a poor standard of play and I was invited back for another game. I went back and had played another good game enjoying it and hoping I had done enough. After a few weeks I received a letter saying that they were just taking on local players due to finances, I thought why did they bother sending me a letter in the first place. About 2 months later when I had signed for Morecambe Academy I received a letter from Exeter offering me a YTS. I was enjoying Morecambe so I declined the offer. At the time when I was going on trials I was desperate for a YTS thinking if you could get 1 you were set for good. Now I have seen that it doesn't matter at all if you are a YTS even at a Premier club in the reserve teams it doesn't mean anything. Only first team games matter most of the time to other clubs if you get released although it is a massive advantage if you can get in with a pro club from an early age.

CHAPTER 4

<u>HOW DID I END UP IN MORECAMBE!</u>

IT IS FUNNY WHEN I think of how I ended up at Morecambe from Guernsey. My friend Scott Bradford had just finished his YTS at Preston North End and due to him being injured towards the end of the season the club gave him another month the following year to come back fit. He started pre-season with them and he managed to get me in to train with them also. I was nearly 17 now and I new it was now or never to get over to England and it would be easier to find a club if I was living there so I moved into Scott's house with his mum and dad Charlie and Tanya in Blackpool, Thornton Cleveleys. It wasn't a trial at Preston really and I had no games I was just there to get fit but obviously if I do well you never know, I thought. We trained with the reserve and youth teams and did some extra running work with the physio Mick Rathbone who is now with Everton. We were there for the month and when Scott left so did I. Scott wrote to loads of clubs in England, Scotland and Ireland with no joy and I was seeing how hard it was to get a club even if you had already completed a YTS which I hadn't.

We started playing for a local side called Squires Gate who were playing in the North West Counties division 2 at the time. The manager Gordon Fell had rang Scott up to play and he got me down too. I played 2 games for Squires Gate in pre-season friendly matches and enjoyed them. Scott then had a call from Sean Gallagher who was a youth coach and a scout at Morecambe FC who were in the Nationwide Conference at the time and are now in League 2. He asked Scott to go down for a trial with the reserves; I went down to watch him it was against Rossendale away. The reserve teams at non- league clubs are made up of trialists, first team players who need games and young lads from the youth team. Scott had done well but they were messing him around a bit and he got a bit disheartened by it all and left.

At the game I got chatting to a coach there and he mentioned that Morecambe were starting an academy up and I should go down for a trial. I went down there and trained for 2 weeks, I had done enough and they signed me on.

The first team manager Jim Harvey was taking the academy that was full time training accompanied with full time education at the Lancaster and Morecambe College. I was delighted and couldn't wait to ring home, after all those trials I was finally getting a chance.

I moved down to Morecambe and shared digs with 5 other lads. There were 18 players in the academy, all of which had just been released from schoolboy forms at professional clubs including Blackburn Rovers, Blackpool, Preston, Rochdale, Bury etc. it was a strong bunch of players who improved leaps and bounds from the moment we started training, all of us had the same thing in common we were all rejected by pro clubs and this was the time to prove people wrong and have one more shot at becoming a professional footballer.

We played for the college team on a Wednesday in the English schools competition. The final we got to that year after playing loads of matches to get there. The final was played at the Hawthorns Stadium, which is home to West Bromich Albion. I met the lads at the ground as I had just flown back from Northern Ireland after getting called up for the under 18 squad to play in a game against the Ukraine in Belfast. I was on the bench and didn't get on but had a good 3 days training, we lost that game 1 0 in Belfast.

The pitch was brilliant at West Brom where we played against Cirencester academy who were highly rated around the colleges. The game didn't go to plan and we lost a game we should of won comfortably, 2 1 the game ended. I was gutted after all the hard work throughout the season to get to the final and harder games which were tougher and more physical than the final, we didn't produce the goods. I enjoyed the academy, the training was first class. With Jim being one of the best coaches in non-league football we were fortunate. I had a grant off of the Guernsey states which helped me enormously in that first year, because we were not being paid by the club. It was a lot of money for parents who's boys were staying in digs during the week and it was difficult for some of the lads who lived further away to travel back home at weekends.

The first digs I stayed in was a big house on the promenade in Morecambe which was run by an elderly couple the man was called Stan and they had a dog which had mange which we tried to avoid contact with at all costs, it lived in the kitchen. The house wasn't in the best of conditions and if it was run as a guesthouse would have certainly not of passed suitable for renting rooms. Dave Edge the Morecambe physiotherapist who was a teacher at the college knew the couple and got us there, it was 40 pound a week for the room without food. When my mum came to see me she cried when she left me there, it wasn't a very nice place but all the lads were staying as well. There was about 6 of us staying there and it was a good mix of personalities living together, we had some laughs living at Stanley's place. We had a curfew of 11 so a couple of times a week we would go down to the Smugglers Den pub which was on the corner down the road and have a few pints then we would go next door for chips and rush back in before 11.

Nick Coyle was our captain and was living in digs with us, He would keep us entertained most of the time with jokes and impressions, and he was great at them William Wallace was his favourite one from the film Braveheart before he went into battle. On Sundays we had a game for Morecambe in the academy league which we won the first year and second I think, the games were against other non-league sides academy's such as Altrincham, Lancaster, Southport, Marine. We also played in the FA Youth Cup one year where I had to miss out on because I was an August birthday and was too old. It was a competitive league in the academy and it was extremely different to what I was used to in Guernsey. We had a good team spirit and were all friends who played for each other. In training Jim went back to basics with us all and we were learning the game from scratch, from our technique to striking a ball in every way, long balls short passes outside of both feet control. We went through everything and it was thoroughly enjoyable, I looked forward to training.

Chapter 5

Trials For Northern Ireland At Lilleshall

ONE OF THE PLAYERS there who was called Matt Spence had a father named Derek Spence, he was a former pro at Blackpool and Bury among others and was also a full international with Northern Ireland. My dad knew Derek from when they were kids growing up in Belfast they lived near each other in Belfast. Matt and I had managed to get a trial with the Northern Ireland under18 set up at Lilleshall. This was only a few months into the academy and we were really excited about this opportunity. The time came when we were to go down for the trials, my family came over and checked in at a hotel down the road from Lilleshall. I met up with the rest of the lads there who were all coming from league clubs and a lot from premier league clubs. It was a bit intimidating but I was looking forward to the challenge. We were here for 3 days and trained and played games against Wolves youth, England under 16s, English schools and Great Britain universities. Matt and I shared a room and next door to us was Mickey Wilson who was from Guernsey. Micky was YTS at Portsmouth and had Irish relations. It was good to see someone else that I knew and I felt more at ease. All of the Irish lads were sound lads anyway so it was easy to get on with people there. Terry Mcflyn was the first lad I spoke to there he came over to chat the first night, Terry is in Australia now playing for the top side Sydney FC, at the time he was at QPR.

I played in 3 games coming on sub at half time. In all 3 games I managed to score. It was a fantastic few days and I exceeded all expectations of myself by scoring in all 3 games and doing more than hold my own with top class players of that age group. Micky had also played solidly all week and deserved to get in the squad but I think they had had the same centre backs for a while.

On the way back up to Morecambe with my family I was buzzing, I said to my dad ive done enough to get in there surely! Especially the fact we had only scored 4 goals in the 3 games. There were games coming up for the European Championships under 18 Qualifiers. I got a letter a few weeks later and it said I was on stand-by for the upcoming game, I was a bit gutted purely because I had played above my weight and done well. Before going I wouldn't have expected anything. There was going to be a few games for the qualifiers and I thought there is a chance of getting in at some point.

In the forthcoming months I had been placed on stand-by for games against Sweden, Finland and also the milk cup which I was disappointed in not participating in because it is one of the best youth tournaments in the world with teams from all over the world.

I was now breaking into the reserve team squad at Morecambe, which was another step up from the youth team. The reserve manager was Jeff Udall, Jeff was hard on a lot of the lads when you first get to him but he is a good guy, and was trying to help lads to realise how tough it was going to be. When Jim had received the invite for Matt and I to go for these trials he pulled us aside after a training session and wanted us both to sign contracts. I suppose it was in case we done well and got snapped up by another club Morecambe wouldn't get a penny for us. I remember after that conversation with him that I was going to actually start getting paid for playing football. When I went into meet with the club and sort out what I was going to sign I was offered £20 pound basic wage and £30 an appearance in the first team. It was peanuts of course but none of the other lads were getting anything so it was better than nothing and the extra bit helped. I was learning to live on very small amounts and I had to budget every week what I could spend.

There was actually 2 Morecambe academy's at the time, the one in Morecambe which I was at and also in Manchester which Alan Keeling ran, 4 or 5 players from that academy went on to make the first team at Morecambe.

It was near the end of the season when I was called up for the under 18 squad for the game against the Ukraine at Sea View Parade stadium, home of Crusaders an Irish Premier League side. I was well pleased and my family were too, they came over to the game. Seeing my name on teletext for the first time, it had my name in the squad with my club Morecambe next to it. The other lads names and the clubs they played for like Southampton, Spurs, Wolves and West Bromich Albion among others it was funny seeing Morecambe next to them.

I always knew I was good enough to make a living out of playing football and when I was called up for Northern Ireland I thought here is a chance on a big stage to show what I can do. We all met up in London where I had got the train from Morecambe in shirt and tie. The squad were at the train station and we all went to the airport by coach when everyone arrived. The manager of the under 18 and under 21 squads was Roy Miller. I got on well with Roy and his teams were always well organised but id probably say defensive minded as Northern Ireland had been with all their teams over the past couple of years against country's with stronger individual players. We flew over to Belfast and got another coach to the hotel where we would be staying. We arrived at night had a bite to eat and went to bed. The next morning we were up early for breakfast then it was off to the training ground. We had a light session with a bit of possession and shooting then it was back for dinner. After dinner we had a rest and then back to the training ground late afternoon for some more work, set pieces were a favourite of the managers he was well organised on these, because they were important for us defensively and attacking. That was how the routine was on international duty eat sleep train and plenty of fluids, water that is, beer was for after the game.

On the day of the game we trained in the morning, personally I don't like it but I can see the meaning to it going through set-pieces and getting loose before a rest and sleep before the game. The team was read out in the morning and I was on the bench for the game, there were 4 players not even involved so I was pleased to get a shirt. My family were all at the game along with my uncle who lives in Ireland. I didn't make an appearance in the game which was a bit disappointing especially when he brought our right back off and replaced him with another defender after we went 1 0 down, I cant understand why managers do this and lots do it, that was how the score stayed.

The next game was Ukraine away in Kiev and I had been selected for this game as well which I was really excited about with Kiev being far from England and knowing we were playing at the massive and historic ground of Dynamo Kiev's. Ukraine being so close to Russia I was expecting it to be freezing cold there but it was lovely sunshine for the four days we were there. When we arrived in Kiev we got the coach to the hotel where we were to be based for the trip. During the journey there seemed to be so many empty buildings and smashed windows, the poverty there was instant to the eye. We arrived to the hotel where as you walked in it felt as though you were going into a time warp going back a hundred years. Every thing about the place was old fashioned with the lifts, the old styled televisions and bedrooms quite run down. I shared a room with Tony Capaldi who was at Birmingham City at the time and then went to Plymouth Argyle FC and now at Cardiff. Tony is a left-sided player with a great left foot and a massive throw. We were the only 2 players in the squad with English accents, the other lads took the Mick out of the English accent but all banter was in good spirit generally. There was always a good bunch of lads in all of the squads I was in.

I struggled with the food in the Ukraine as it consisted of soup that was made of boiling water and raw vegetables and salads. I lived off of fries and plain baguettes for four days. We trained at a local sides training ground it was really hot and humid with mosquito's everywhere. I was trying my hardest to impress and was desperate to get on the pitch especially when we went to see the ground it was amazing. 80,000 all-seated, it was huge you could fit the whole population of Guernsey in there and room for another 3rd. Near the changing rooms you had to walk through a little plaza and church type place before you went on to the pitch, I wish now that I had taken some photos while I was on there. After our training sessions when we got back on the coach there was always lots of kids outside asking for some clothes and boots shin pads or anything we had on. Some of the lads gave them some shorts and socks, the kids were over the moon. The day of the game came and we had a meeting before we went out to train in the morning. I was counting how many players were here and there was one too many for the squad meaning one of us wouldn't be involved, all that way to Ukraine not to be involved. I wasn't the player left out fortunately for me and I was on the bench. On the way to the ground the coach was buzzing and everyone was excited about playing at such a historic stadium. When we arrived at the ground there was lots of policemen with guns and a few supporters there. The pitch was really nice and big but the grass was a little long. The game was played during the day and the temperature was high. Mark Clyde who was at Wolves at the time and has unfortunately retired due to injury now stood out among the rest he had a great game at centre back, he was also one of the youngest players in the team. We were playing really well and were all over the Ukrainians until they had a breakaway goal.

There was about 20 minutes to go when I was told to warm up. I was nervous warming up but was really wanting to get on to the pitch. I was itching to get on even more for the fact that it would be my last chance to be capped at under 18 level, I had got the shout to go back to the bench from warming up. I went on for the last 18 minutes, I felt extremely proud to be running on the pitch at dynamo Kiev's stadium for Northern Ireland, my fathers country and whom I was representing all my family there and my dads friends who were born in Ireland. As soon as I got on there was a corner kick, and the ball fell to me perfectly but I didn't get great connection on the ball, I got enough on it to beat the keeper and it crept over the line. A defender then trying to get the ball clear, whacked it away from behind the line, it was a goal. I was reeling off to celebrate when the next thing the linesman raised his flag, I was furious and ran straight over to him. The goal wasn't given as the linesman said it hadn't crossed the line. My head had gone and I was booked for my protests. It could have been a lot worse when they took a free kick short and when I chased after the ball I caught one of the players heel from behind. As soon as I did it I though oh no I'm off here but I just got a warning luckily. That was my first minute of international football. We fought hard to get an equaliser but it didn't come. I was annoyed at myself after the game that I didn't make better contacted and rushed the shot, you always have more time than you think when you look back at situations on the pitch but at the time I had snatched at it. I was glad that I got capped though and enjoyed the experience. That night the team went into Kiev and had a couple of drinks. There was a festival on at the time and there were hundreds of people in the streets drinking and dancing. There was a great atmosphere in the city centre although we didn't stay out long, after a few hours wondering about and chatting we went back to the hotel.

We flew back to England the next day to London and then the northern-based players flew to Manchester. I had brought a big bottle of vodka back for the rest of lads at our digs, on the flight from London to Manchester there was only a few of us on the flight and the manager wasn't on the plane so we had a few beers. We had planned to go out in Manchester for a night out, but by the time we got back we decided just to travel home to the different places where we were staying. Owen Morrison who was at Sheffield Wednesday was involved in the first team and he needed to get back. When we got our bags I bumped into one of the lads with my trolley and the extra big vodka bottle smashed everywhere on the floor. The lads at digs didn't believe my story though.

CHAPTER 6

AN ACCIDENT SHAVING

I GOT THE TRAIN back to Morecambe from the airport, its about an hour and a half, the whole train journey I was thinking about that chance I had to score and asking myself why didn't I concentrate better on the ball and anticipate the ball arriving to me. I was thinking I could have been travelling back up to my club having scored a goal for my country. A few situations have arisen in my career that were similar to the chance I had in Kiev but I guess its just one of those things where you make a decision at that moment and you haven't a lot of time to think about it. I got a taxi back to my digs from the train station but all of the lads had gone home for the weekend, they would go back home on weekends to Blackpool, Preston and to other places all over Lancashire. I stayed in digs on my own in the holidays and at weekends at first which was hard at times and got a bit boring. Sometimes I would stay with one of the lad's family's. I used to stay at Danny Crumblehumes house in Blackpool and at Perks house in Heyshem, both of their family's were really nice and welcomed me when ever I stayed. Stan the man who was my landlord in the digs where I was at was a very keen chess player, he taught me how to play the game, I really enjoyed it and still do when I meet someone else who plays. I used to play him a lot when know one else was there and

I improved, that was all there was to do.

One day in digs things turned sour for me at Stans. I was having a shave up in my room that was at the top of the building, a couple of the lads were down stairs beneath me playing on the computer, pro evolution soccer which we played all of the time. The water went off whilst I was starting to have a shave so I just left the room and went downstairs with the lads. I was just beating Matt on pro evolution when some water came straight through the light bulb. All of us in the room shot up and I raced upstairs only to see that my bedroom had flooded. The tap had come back on whilst I was down stairs and I had forgotten to take the plug out. The owners of the digs went berserk and threw me out that night. The fire engines were called out, so I just left and went down to the pub down the road to get out of the way. Not knowing what to do I spoke to a couple of the other lads Alty and Taff who were staying at the York hotel, they had a word with the landlord there so I moved in to the York that night. £40 a week it was at the York and the people were friendly enough although the place was a bit rough at times, there was never any hassle there with us. Credit to the lads at my other digs when I got kicked out they all moved out so they all ended up joining the rest of us at the York hotel. There were 3 of us in each room and it was a good crack, there was a snooker table there too, which was good. After the season had finished I went back to Guernsey for the summer.

It was a nice feeling going home now that I had found a club in England and that I was going back after the break. It was also great to see my mates again like Dan Cavanaugh and Paul Van Beek who have been mates for years after we all met playing for Archenoul Decor whose coach was Dan's dad Charlie. We were always playing basketball when we were younger and Dan had a court in his garden which we were up till after midnight most nights in the holidays playing 2 vs. 2 and 1 vs. 1 after Charlie had put floodlights in. I have done a bit of work for Charlie a couple of times in the summers when he's had some labouring jobs on but he doesn't let me any where near a paintbrush which I struggle to understand. He just doesn't rate me at painting.

Working definitely makes me appreciate playing football for a living and Ive tried never to take it for granted for I know I will not make enough money to retire on, I'm prepared for when the time comes to work. But there is plenty of time to work and I will enjoy playing football whilst I'm making a living from it.

I came back to pre-season training raring to go, id done a lot of running whilst I was back home in the summer. Thinking I might get a sniff of the first team, a few of us were invited back to training early with the first team. It was really hard for the first couple of weeks like most pre-seasons are. It's getting the stamina training in at first the longer running and then building up to the short stuff. Morecambe was still a part-time club but the academy was full-time. The first team was training three times a week and the standard was a big step up from the youth team. I felt comfortable with it during training and then into matches, I was involved in all the pre-season friendly games against the likes of Blackburn Rovers, Crewe, Wolves, Oldham, Preston, Blackpool and there was Scottish teams like Gretna and Morton that came down. That year it was Blackburn and Crewe who were the big games, I played in both and done well.

There were also games against non-league opposition just to get that type of physical game because playing premiership teams and then playing in the conference was completely different games. The better teams let you play and pass the ball around before closing you down where as non-league football you don't get a lot of time on the ball as you are closed down by the nearest man.

I had done well in pre-season and made the squad for the first game of the season at home to Rushden & Diamonds. It was a good feeling and I was excited at the prospect of getting on in a big game at our stadium. Rushden were the bookies favourites for promotion as they spent a lot of money that year, one of their signings was Justin Jackson who they had brought for £180,000 from Morecambe. The owner of Doctor Martins was the chairman and it is a terrific set up at Nene Park. There was over 2000 at the game and the atmosphere was great I was warming up with a big smile. I was18 the week before the game and I was just going into my second year as a youth team player. I had made quick improvements over the year to my game under the guidance of Jim Harvey. I came on as sub to make my first team debut with about 20 minutes to go I was nervous but got a few touches and did ok although didn't set the game a light. I did have an embarrassing moment as with one of my first touches the ball was played long to me and I didn't know whether to control the ball on my chest or head it, I did neither and ended up hand balling it. After that game I was involved in the squad now and then but mainly in the reserves where I was a regular now.

It wasn't until the last 12 games of the season that I was in the squad regularly and I came on in every one of those 12 games. During the season I was training during the days with the academy and then at nights with the first team. My position was just behind the front striker and in front of the midfield. This is my best position and I enjoyed playing here and getting on the ball linking things between the midfield and striker, Jim Harvey's sides always play in that way 4-4-1-1. I think it's a great formation and it always encourages the team to play passing football and through midfield.

In the first team at this time the player in my position was John Norman who had done well for Morecambe for a number of years. He was a good footballer who wasn't quick but was very clever and a quick thinker, John helped me out a lot during training and talked a lot to me about the game. When I was in the first team however, I was always played on the right or left wing. I was coming on sub with about 30 minutes to go and was doing really well creating chances and I set up a lot of goals.

CHAPTER 7

MALTA

WE WERE PLAYING KINGSTONIAN away at their place when I got a call up for the Northern Ireland Under 21 squad to play away in Malta. I was one of the youngest in the squad and it was a surprise to get the call up, I was made up though. I had a good game at Kingstonian when I came on at half time I set up one goal and we won 1 0. I got a lift after the game to meet up with the Irish squad, at the hotel near the airport. I didn't arrive there till late so didn't see any of the lads till the morning for breakfast.

When I met the other lads I saw Chris Tardif a goalkeeper from Guernsey and a friend I used to play with when we were at Vale Rec as kids. He was at Portsmouth at the time and he was in the squad as cover for Elliot Morris, it was great to see him there. Being born in Guernsey you can choose to represent any of the home nations in sport as well as France. Many thought that Matt Le Tissier would have chosen to represent France before England as they probably would have suited his style of play and he may have won more caps for them. He deserved more caps for England in my opinion some of the goals he was scoring on a regular basis and the unique style of which he used to play, people paid to watch him and he entertained supporters.

Malta is a beautiful country and I had a great trip. It was really hot over there and we stayed in a lovely hotel with a swimming pool on the roof top. This is the life I was thinking gazing out to the harbour on the roof top. If the boys could see me now back at Morecambe, We had the usual training regime and Roy's methods were the same each trip. The team was named in the pre-match meeting in the morning where he would place the team and formation along with the subs up on a board. I was named as a sub and was happy to be involved but wanted to get a game of course. We arrived at the stadium on match day and it was a nice little stadium, it was near the end of the season in the Maltese league too, so the pitch wasn't as great as it would have been earlier on in the season. Apparently all the games in the league over there are played at this one stadium.

My mum and dad had their honeymoon in Malta, they told me that there last 70 pound they had left went on a pair of football boots for my dad who played a couple of games for a local side there. They are very friendly people the locals in Malta, I would definitely go back to Malta, nice place. We lost the game 1-0, but the team played well and should of got something out of the game, it was the last game for a lot of the players as it was the last game in the European championship qualifiers where they had failed to qualify for. I didn't get on which was a little disappointing but the manager said I trained well and that I would be definitely involved again, that pleased me. After the game we had a few beers in the hotel before flying back to England the next day, good trip.

When I got back from Malta we had a couple of games left which I was again involved in and beginning to make an impact on the team. We finished the season in 3rd position the highest ever for Morecambe, there was no play-off then just top team went up and that was it. I went back home after the season had finished and I found a lot of people were following my progress which was nice. Most people are very supportive in Guernsey and wish me well when I see them, there are some that don't like to see people do well and get kicks out of bad news but that's definitely a minority. The conference was fast changing and becoming a well respected league with lots of players moving into the league. It can be a mentality of people to watch matches on television or from the sidelines and say this is a crap standard I could play at this level! All footballers who play professionally realise how difficult it is moving up the leagues. I must admit though watching some of my games on DVD thinking that was a great game of football before I put it on then after watching it back thinking that was absolutely crap. When I come back to Guernsey and am out I sometimes get people come up to me and will say so and so should be playing in the football league or conference standard easy. Its hard to answer that without upsetting people but realistically its one thing looking brilliant at amateur level but when your playing with players that are just as good if not better a lot of the time its not all about ability, everything comes into playing football, attitude and mental strength and confidence are just some, but there is no doubt that there are players over here given a chance could play at a higher level. The higher up in the leagues you go the easier it can get in regards to having more time on the ball, the difference being when you do get the ball you have to make a positive pass or keep possession because when the ball is lost the other team wont be giving it back lightly and you have to work hard to retain possession of the ball. Players that are at the highest level are there for a reason and they deserve to be where they are although even the top players come under criticism, and that goes for every league criticism is just part and parcel of the game.

When I left Guernsey I said to myself that whatever level I play at as long as I give it my best shot and don't have any regrets ill be happy whatever level I reach as long as im making a living from the game and am playing to the highest ability I can.

I don't want to be a person in the pub at 50 saying I could have been, and could of made it if. I want to be able to say that I gave it my best and I played at whatever level I will play because that's where I was good enough to play, or even better not to have to say anything and let my football do all the talking for me. For me I don't think it matters what standard of football you play as long as you're true to yourself and have enjoyed playing the beautiful game, as Pele would gracefully say.

At the end of the season I signed a 1year contract with a year option. It was the year Morecambe was going full time, all of the younger players and some of the senior players were full time with the rest still coming on the 2 nights and try and make a couple of days if they could get time off work. We trained days and then joined the rest for the 2 nights. It was a lot of training but we would get days off or the odd night so it was ok. I had a pay rise to £120 a week and £1000 signing on fee. I had been in digs in the west end of Morecambe with the academy lads that were a year below me, it was ok one of the women lecturers and her girlfriend ran the guesthouse they were both in their 50s, until one of the lads Carl Stanford came back after a few beers at Maggie's bar in west end he had an argument with them and they punched him both of them. We couldn't believe it when we got back so I said im moving out because he was being thrown out. I was with my mate Nasher at the time when we saw Carl and Nash asked if I wanted to stay at his place where he was staying with a friend and his mum Barbara at 28 central drive. His mate Matt was a physical training instructor in the army. His mum was Barbara who owned the house she was a lovely lady and her partner Weldon who lived there also. I lived there for 2 and a half years altogether and it was very homely there I was happier at Barbara's than any other of my digs before. The rest of the lads found new digs as well I think they weren't happy at what had happened and the women were regretful at how they had reacted. Probably more regretful at the money they would be losing out on with us all moving out. Michel Knowles (Nash) was in the first team at Morecambe and I met him whilst he was doing some training with us while coming back from injury.

Pre-season was as tough as usual but again I had looked after myself in the summer as most players do now days. Our first friendly was against Wigan Athletic at their new ground called the JJB stadium this was the first game to be played on the new stadium before Man United opened it officially the week after. The pitch was amazing like a bowling green and it had been raining so the pitch was perfect. We played really well and I played the last 15 minutes, we drew the game 0 0, my mum and sister were at the game and 8,000 were watching. Other friendlies were against Blackburn like every year and Wolves were the other big team with Paul Ince, Dennis Irwin and Henri Camara in the team, we drew with Wolves

3-3 and I scored a cracker. After the first 5 league games of the season I was given my first start, I was on the lefty wing and I had a good solid debut. It was a good feeling walking out onto the pitch from the start and getting clapped on by the fans I really enjoyed it and we won the game. That season I went on to play in most of the games and was a regular playing on the left or right wing and also as a second striker. I started 35 games and came on as sub for the rest scoring 8 goals from midfield. We didn't do that great in the league but we had good cup runs. We got to the quarterfinals in the FA trophy and the 3rd round of the FA Cup.

CHAPTER 8

FA CUP

As a conference side we entered the FA cup in the 4th round qualifier. We were drawn against Bridlington Terriers a team from the North East who had won there league lots of times but couldn't gain promotion due to there ground not meeting a criteria. We would see just why when we arrived there on a cold winter's day pouring down with rain. It was a pitch just surrounded by a barrier and the pitch was in a right mess due to the heavy raining they had up there, we had prepared for them being a physical side and a bit nasty and we weren't disappointed it was probably the most physical game ive played in and some of the more experienced players had said the same. I started on the right hand side of midfield this game and I remember having my head shaved the day before the game. Whilst we were warming up the crowd was coming in and it seemed like a few thousand were watching but it was probably just over 1,000 watching. But because of there being a tiny stand and the rest stood up there seemed a lot more, they were a extremely hostile crowd too I could see why teams were getting intimidated coming here. We were getting some stick off of them getting called all the names under the sun. Despite the conditions and crowd we started the game really well and were knocking the ball past them with ease.

Garry Thompson scored a cracking left foot shot, then we scored again. Tackles were really starting to fly in and they weren't happy at the way we were passing around them. Bridlington managed to pull a goal back with about 10 minutes to go and we were hanging on now after being comfortable. With 2 minutes to go John Norman broke free and had a shot that rebounded off of the post and fell to me as I was backing him up and I passed it into the empty net, 3-1. We were glad to get out of that place and I dread getting drawn against them in the cups. I remember the manager having a go at one of the lads for having blades on in such a muddy pitch and I was hiding my blades under a top so he couldn't see them. The next round we were drawn against Forest Green Rovers who also play in the conference.

Mean while I had been called up for the Under 21 squad for 2 fixtures to face Spain away in Valencia and the Ukraine at Ballymena showground's in Northern Ireland. It was 2 big games to be called in to and I was excited at the prospect of playing against some of the Spanish players who were some of the best young talent in Europe and were already playing first team football at there clubs. Ariel Arteta who was at Glasgow Rangers and Fernando Torres were the big 2 players. I met up with the Irish squad in London after getting the train down. We flew to Valencia went straight to the hotel to put our bags in and then we went out on the coach along the coast and stopped off at the beach. It was out of season and there was no-one around, the sun was out and it was beautiful to see so much beach with nobody on it. We trained at a really nice venue on a local ground the pitch was perfect and I had a really good 3 days training probably the best out of all my trips away with the squads. I was playing a lot of first team football at Morecambe I was more confident in my ability and I was probably only 1 of a handful in the squad that were playing first team football. We had a good squad and on the day of the game I was named as a sub. It was a great feeling on the coach to the game everyone was well up for this game and although I was sub I was part of it. When we arrived at the stadium there were a couple of hundred fans waiting for us to get off of the coach, there were video cameras and the people wanted autographs. It was very surreal and was a very different experience.

We walked into the stadium and on to the pitch, the stadium was called Amensa and is a stadium especially for the Spanish under 18's and under 21's National sides.

The place was packed out there must have been 10,000 in attendance and it was an overwhelming atmosphere, it was good just warming up before and half time, which unfortunately was all the action I got.

The pitch was like a bowling green it was artificial grass but soft, the lads had played brilliantly and kept the score at 0-0 right up until the last minute. When Arteta had a free kick and Tony Capaldi unfortunately deflected the ball with a header into his own net, the whistle blew for full time one minute later.

Everybody was disappointed because the lads had worked hard the whole game, but Spain were awesome and I have never seen a team keep the ball for such long periods and be so patient in their build up play. The ball was hardly in the air the whole game apart from when we tried to clear the ball away.

Sammy McIlroy was the first team manager at the time and at the end of the game he came into the changing rooms and told us he was very impressed, he called a few of the players up for the senior squad against Spain in a friendly in Ireland.

After the game we had a couple of beers in the hotel, then flew back to England the next day.

It was great being involved in the trip, training and playing in different countries and meeting up with the Northern Ireland squads which were always enjoyable and was good to meet up with players from different teams and see some familiar faces.

The Ukraine game was the week after in Ballymena.

When I got back to Morecambe I had a game before going to Northern Ireland which I was sub for because I missed a game whilst I was away and we had won therefore the manager kept the same team.

Jim Harvey had recently been appointed Northern Ireland's assistant manager to MacIlory, which was good for me.

Jim and Sammy were big pals and it helped me as Jim could see my progress and could then report back to Sammy and the under 21 coach, but there were not many games left for me in that squad as there were not many qualifiers yet.

At the game against Ukraine I was named as sub, Jim came into the changing rooms before the game to wish me all the best which I really apprciated, I had yet to be capped for the under 21's even though I had been in the squad a couple of times, so I was eager to earn my first cap. I did earn my cap that day as I came on for the last 25 minutes, unfortunately I didn't feel that I played to my potential that game. I remember feeling really disappointed with myself because I had trained so well in both Spain and Belfast and felt really fit, but this happens sometimes especially when you come on as sub, I was ready to be playing at this level however I felt I didn't make the most of a chance.

My Uncle Pat, Auntie Bridget and my Granddad were at the game that day and I stayed with them in Ballymena after the game. We had a couple of beers and caught up as I hadn't seen a lot of them in the recent years.

Chapter 9

GERMANY AT WINDSOR PARK

THE BEST GAME I played for Northern Ireland was for the Under 21's against Germany at Windsor Park in a friendly match, I was called up for the game after being on standby.

I was training really well for the 2 days in Belfast and was now one of the more experienced players, it was a shame that my family couldn't get over from Guernsey to see the game, but my family in Ireland came.

Windsor Park is where Northern Ireland have played their home Internationals for many years and has a lot of history, I remember my dad talking about it, watching matches there when he was younger with the great George Best and Pat Jennings gracing the field. It is also the home to Linfield who play in the Irish Premier League.

On the day of the game, the team was picked in the morning as usual and on the team sheet my name was next to the number shirt. So this was my first start for Northern Ireland and it was to be against Germany wearing my favourite shirt number 10, where I would be playing as a striker.

The build up to the game seemed really long and all I wanted to do was get on the pitch, we always had a pre match dinner a few hours before kick off, but I didn't eat that much that day.

Walking out onto the pitch I was proud to be wearing the green and white shirt, even though I wasn't born there I felt I was that day. I was also playing for my dad, his family and friends.

When we got onto the pitch before kick off, the starting 11 and the German starting 11 were lined up for the National Anthems.

The game was live on TV in Germany and when it was our Anthem, the cameraman came very close to you on the line, player by player, It was a strange feeling to have a camera that close and knowing that it was live on TV. I have watched it on TV on International games when the camera zooms in on the players during the National Anthem but I never realised that they came that close.

The game kicked off and I started really well with my first touch being a good one, I found when I had a good first touch in the game I thought that I would usually play well.

The German team were a massive team, every player must have been over 6 foot with the exception of their captain Thomas Hitzlesberger, who was the best player on the park, and he was at Aston Villa at the time but hadn't been a regular in their team until after this game where his manager was watching in the stand.

Hitzlesberger had a great left foot, the rest of the German side played in the Bundesliga.

I felt really confident in this game and I was linking up well with the rest of the team and had a few good runs, taking on the German defenders and getting a couple of shots off, I should have scored when I played a lovely one two, with our midfielder and I walked past one of the defenders with ease, to go one on one with the goalkeeper who made a craeking save tipping the ball around the post, I should have scored though.

I had 2 really good chances that game and created a couple and although we ended up losing 1-0, we deftnitely deserved a draw.

After the game a lot of the lads were exchanging shirts and unlike the Spain game when I tried to swap my shirt and no one would take it I didn't want to swap my shirt this game as I had number 10. After the game I was pleased with my performance and I thought if scouts were watching I would have to be in with a chance, especially being the only non-league player playing International football at under 21 level. I had heard a few rumours that a couple of clubs were going to table a bid for me but I didn't hear anything from it.

The Germany game was to be my last Under 21 match as I was out of the age group at this game. I was involved with one more game and that was Sammy Macllorys testimonial game, which was Northern Ireland B squad Vs Macclesfield Town were he was manager for and gained promotional from the Conference with them. I was pleased to be invited to the game but was disappointed when I found out whilst I was on the bench, that was my club hadn't insured me for the match so I couldn't go on, even though I was sub. I was called up late for the game and they messed up my insurance, I was fuming after the game because it was a good opportunity to play at B level.

I thoroughly enjoyed my time playing for Northern Ireland and was now thinking ahead to the senior team, although I knew I would have to be playing extremely well at club level or to get a move to get into the football league.

The first round of the FA cup was against Forest Green Rovers away.

A couple of weeks before the game the team had been told that we were going away for a couple of day on a mid season break.

Morecambe had a new Chairman who was part owner of Umbro called Peter Maguigan and the club had also won the fair play award the previous season, therefore we got a cash sum for it.

The trip was to La Manga in Spain and we were staying at the same hotel as were the England team stay for their training camps.

We had had a good start to the season before this and a win at Forest Green would see us into the second round for the FA cup, and would make the trip all the better.

We won the game 2-1 and one of their players had scored one of the best own goals of all time which still gets repeated on TV. I had crossed the ball into the box and the defender who had plenty of time to clear the ball smashed it into his own net, right in the top corner.

We didn't play particular well that game but worked hard to get a win, in their bar after the game we were all glued to the TV to watch the draw for the second round.

We were drawn at home to Cambridge United who were at the time in League 1.

But first we were off to La Manga for a few days training. We didn't get much training done we were at the bar most of the trip, It was a great laugh although I got ill on the last day, it was really hot there so we were either at the swimming pool or the lads that played golf were on the course all day. We did have a run one day in the morning that I was late for, we all had hangovers and everyone struggled in the heat. When we arrived back to England we had a bad run in the league and lost a few games on the spin.

Chapter 10

<u>TAXI</u>

CHRISTMAS WAS COMING UP and I wanted to get back home to see my family for a couple of days. In the conference fixtures it was hard to get home because the Christmas period is a busy time with a game on Boxing Day then the Saturday and new years day. The games were normally against local teams closest to you so there would generate more fans through the turnstiles. We play Southport on Boxing Day and again on New Year's Day. I flew back to Guernsey for Christmas from Manchester airport but had to get a return flight to Birmingham on Boxing Day. Id planned to get a train to Morecambe early so I could get the bus up with the team. Up until Christmas id played every game apart from one or two and was doing well. In Guernsey I spent a few days at home seeing all of the family and caught up with friends. Boxing Day came and I got the early bird flight to Birmingham and headed straight to the train station, but there were no trains to the north west of England today. I was starting to panic there had also been a delay getting my bag back off of the plane so time was ticking. I rang my dad and he said just to get a taxi and he would pay for it. So I went to the taxi rank and asked for a taxi to Southport because I had no time to get to Morecambe first. The driver said it would be £180 and showed me his price list, I went to ask a few more and they said the same price. I went back to the first driver and got in with him. It was taking forever to get to Southport, I didn't realise how far away it was from Birmingham and I knew I was going to be late for the game. It wouldn't have been as bad but the second round of the FA cup was in a couple of weeks.

The manager was on the phone and I explained to him the situation. I arrived 50 minutes before kick off and the team had been named I wasn't in the squad. Nasher came into the team for me on the right wing. It was in this game where he suffered a horrific injury; he fractured his hip and dislocated his pelvis in a freak accident in where he tripped on a divot on the pitch and had his foot stuck in it. It wasn't a tackle and no one was near him. I can't remember the score just nashers injury. He was in hospital for a while and it was hard seeing a friend and team mate get such an injury. He done brilliantly coming back from that injury and played a season at Accrington Stanley when he gained fitness. He tells people the scar on his leg is a shark bite and regularly gets it out on a night out. On New Years Day it was Southport at home and I was back in the team but I had been feeling the effects of my break in Guernsey and I didn't play that well with the Cambridge game coming up it was touch and go whether I was going to start. The build up to the game was great and our whole team was buzzing I had been getting a lot of publicity and some write ups in the local papers as well as shoot magazine, for being voted in the top ten strikers in the conference, and In Match magazine for being a player to look out for. There were reports in the papers that 4 or 5 of us at Morecambe were being watched by Liverpool, Blackburn and Man City. It was a nice thing to see but how true it was I don't know. We had a very young team with five or six of us coming through into the first team to become regulars with a further one or two academy graduates making the bench.

CHAPTER 11

MATCH OF THE DAY

THE GAME WAS TO be shown as featured highlights on Match of the Day. I couldn't wait for that and for all my friends and family in Guernsey to watch me play on TV. I always watched Match of the Day growing up so I was excited to think I would be on there too. I was now praying that I would be in the starting 11, thankfully on the day of the game after our pre match meal I was named in the team. I was starting on the left wing, we got to Christie Park and the atmosphere was electric, from the time we warmed up to the final whistle our fans were singing and encouraging their team. We started brightly and I was drifting inside and getting involved in the game. Cambridge United was 2 divisions higher than Morecambe but the cup is a leveller and a neutral wouldn't have told the difference. We scored first from a corner John Hardiker claimed the goal and was interviewed after the game, he went up for a header along with John Norman who also claimed the goal, I think they both got a bit of the ball. We were dominating the game and had a couple more chances but didn't put them away. Then they equalised, we were a bit shook up by there goal and they were putting us under pressure just before half time.

The whistle blew for half time and it was 1-1. I was feeling ok but had drifted out of the game a little. We were playing well so the manager just told us to keep playing our game passing and moving. We started the first half as we did the second putting them under pressure and I was getting involved more but didn't have any chances on goal. After 75minutes the manager changed things around and I came off along with 2 others. Mark Quayle had come on the pitch and he was to be our hero when he was put through 1 on 1 with the keeper and slotted a brilliant finish underneath the goalkeeper. 2-1 it stayed, we were through to the FA Cup 3rd round the highest round in the clubs history. It was a brilliant day, after the game the newspaper Mirror was in our changing rooms as the beer and champagne was getting drunk we were singing whilst the photos were being taken. When I got the papers the next day though I was gutted when I saw that our kit man Tom Sawyer had marked me out of every photo in the Sun newspaper, Mirror and People there was Tom standing in front of me. The lads were laughing with that.

Some of us that lived locally went out after the game into town and had a night out. It was a great day, now we were wandering who we were going to play in the next round, Liverpool, Man UTD, Arsenal any of those three would be nice, I was just hoping for a premier league side it didn't really matter who but obviously the big 3 are always the teams that everyone wants to play. I watched the 3rd round draw on a big screen in walkabout bar in Lancaster; we were the next ones out of the hat after Arsenal who drew Farnborough Town from the same league as us. We drew Ipswich town FC who at the time were lying 3rd in the Premiership and remained in that position for a number of months and a team which were full of international players. It was a massive draw for us and everyone at the club was delighted with the chance to play a premier league club in 1 of the greatest cup competitions in the world.

Leading up to this game was unbelievable, it was like being a premiership player for a week leading up to the game, obviously without the wages. We did have a nice little cup bonus after the Ipswich game mind, over a grand each for the 4 cup games. But the publicity we got was amazing and with my name Zico I got even more interviews and photos with all the big newspapers and local papers from Manchester, Preston areas. One interview was with Sky Sports News, it was on the pitch at Christie Park I had my training kit on and the interviewer was asking me questions about myself and I was answering him while keeping the ball up in the air then passing back the ball back to him in the air and so forth. It was funny watching it back although a little embarrassing. Another interview and photo shoot was funny, I was out training with all of the team and there was lots of cameras there and photographers, they came over and they all wanted to talk to me about where I got my name from etc. So there I was talking and getting photos taken whilst all of the lads were training. I got some stick off of them after training; I had a picture taken for the Manchester Evening News holding the FA Cup, which was special holding the famous cup. I was never going to lift it so this would be the closest id get. It wasn't just me getting the interviews though and on the day of the game we were at the same restaurant having our pre-match meal and on the television was our centre midfield player Steve Walters who supported Ipswich and our goalkeeper Mark Smith, they played out a sketch of Morecambe and Wise which was shown on bbc1 football focus, it was hilarious and great to calm everyone's nerves before the match. I also had interviews on the radio with radio 1 and some other regional and national stations which was fun. The day of the game came around quick time after the draw was made and with it being played at our home ground It was going to be extra special. The atmosphere was electric and was even better than the Cambridge game which was also good. I was named number 11 on the left wing up against there right back Sylvain Wilnes the Dutch full back. Warming up seeing the crowds packing in to the ground got everyone right up for the game and we wanted to put on a show. Although we weren't very consistent in the league we had a team that on our day could beat most teams and we were confident of getting a draw without playing negatively which we couldn't play even if we wanted to. We knew they were a good side and especially in midfield and attacking they were strong Marcus Stewart was banging in the goals for them that season and was up there among the leading goal scorers in the Premiership. Matt Holland was there main man in the midfield along with the experienced Jim Magilton. It was a really quick game with there fitness being exceptional and our adrenalin pumping hard and keeping the pace with them. We kept the ball fairly well and early on Tomo went on a great run and fired the ball across goal which I had made a well timed run to lose my marker at the back post. The ball came to me about the penalty spot out and I took a touch instead of hitting it first time. By the time I had my first touch Richard Wright there goalkeeper was out to me like lightning and smothered the ball. It was a great opportunity which haunted me for weeks especially when I seen it on television in the night. The worst thing is we played Burscough in the FA Trophy the week after and the exact same thing happened and I hit the ball first time and scored. After that scare for them they picked up there game and were playing good stuff. They scored with big Alan Armstrong scoring a header. We gave them a good game and didn't shame ourselves with the final result being 3-0. I got Marcus Stewarts shirt after the game and there was a big marquis outside the ground with food and drink. All of my family had come over to watch the game so we had a lot of drink and some food in the night. It was my biggest game in club football but I am hoping it won't be my last big game like that. That's the beauty of the FA Cup you can be your average lower league player and be drawn on to the big stage against some of the best players in the world and be a star footballer for a game.

That season could have ended in disaster though with all our cup successes as we got to the semi finals of the FA Trophy and got knocked out by Stevenage Borough but beat a lot of teams before it. We narrowly avoided relegation and played Hereford on one of the last games of the season where we escaped by other teams losing and us drawing I think. That season was a great one with the FA Cup making it a special season and I was really pleased with establishing myself in the team and making the amount of appearances.

CHAPTER 12

A NEW SEASON

I WENT HOME FOR the summer and was doing some part-time work at Beausejour leisure centre in Guernsey and was working a bit with my mate's dad Charlie doing some labouring. I wasn't getting paid in the summer so I needed to keep ticking over with some cash. Id trained quite hard over the summer running on the cliffs and track whilst keeping a weight training programme. When pre-season started I was ready for it and was relaxed as I was on contract still. There were always a lot of trialists at pre-season players that are either out of contract at their former clubs or have been released, there are normally a lot of YTS that are on trial as so many do get released every year. That year Jim had brought in a lot of experienced players to complement the younger lads. Chris Lightfoot, Ian Arnold, Andy Gouck, later on he brought in David Lee who was with Bolton and Southampton. Dave was an old fashioned right winger and was very quick in his prime and although he was exceptionally fit, he told me he runs every morning at 6am the same run every day, at Morecambe he obviously didn't have the kind of pace he did have but played in the same style looking to take his man on the outside and get a cross in. I remember playing against Tony Daley a few times when he was at Forest Green and he was the same sort of player, I was on the left wing and he was on the right, he was also a little older but still fit I wouldn't have fancied marking him in his hay day though he was rapid. In pre-season we were looking the part and had hammered a Blackpool first team 5-0 and had drawn with a Wolves first team 3-3 I had scored 2 crackers in those games Wolves shad Paul Ince playing along with Dennis Irwin, Henri Camera and Luzhny the old Arsenal right back and there captain Butler among other names. We also had a 0-0 draw with a strong Blackburn side, I had a particularly good game playing up front with big Wayne Curtis and did everything but put the ball in the net which of course is the hardest thing to do, I remember going in for a tackle with Egil Ostenstad and just bouncing off him. We had a good mixture of ages in our squad but found that our main players and our most experienced were getting injured a lot that year and we had an up and down season although we finished the season strongly. Robbie Talbot and Adriano Rigoglioso had signed and Rob had a great year being our leading goal scorer and lots of teams were looking at him before he suffered a nasty injury which kept him out for a long time. They were both great lads and we had a lot of laughs, I was in and out of the team and had had a bit of a falling out with Jim which I think he never really forgave me for.

I was in good form and had been approached by an agent to meet him. I went for dinner in Liverpool to speak to him and he was confident that some league clubs wanted to sign me and he could help me when I move on. I always wanted to improve and was excited that I could move into the league. I signed up with him but had told him that I had already agreed a 3 year contract with Morecambe. I had already received 1000 pound as part of a signing on fee but my basic wage wasn't good. He asked me if id signed anything and I told him that I hadn't. He then told me that a league club was ready to sign me if I could get out of my contract and since I hadn't put pen to paper I wasn't signed. So I went into Jim's office and told him that I had signed on with an agent and that I wanted to play in the football league. That was it Jim went nuts at me and told me to get out of his room, then he stopped me as I walked out and spoke calmly again saying I had made a mistake and what about all that he had done for me, which he had really giving me a chance.

I felt terrible and wasn't sure what to do, my agent had told me that there was someone waiting to sign me and then Jim was telling me to get rid of him and trust him whom id known as my coach for 4 years. What made things worse was Jim's son was an agent and had tried to sign me up with him. I decided to tell my agent I was going to stay at Morecambe and I ended up changing my contract to a 2 year instead of a 3 and had a clause in my contract that if a club made a £100, 000 offer for me I could leave and my agent would get 10%of the fee. The fact was I didn't benefit one little bit and was worse off because Jim had the hump with me for ages and wouldn't play me. From that time on it was up and down with me and the manager. I thought I was doing the right thing but really I should have gone one direction or the other stuck with the agent and took a chance or just ignored it and carried on what I was doing. I spoke with my agent a couple of times then I had lost my phone with all my numbers and couldn't get hold of him so that was it. I had still played a lot of games but was in and out of the team all the time and 7 games on the run was probably the best run I had other than that it was 2 or 3 games then on the bench for a few and so on. I scored a few, 7 in cup and league but compared to the season before it wasn't as good a year for me. We didn't have a run in the cup and we just missed out on the play offs finishing sixth. We were training every day and it was always good but the club was still going through the change of part time to full time and it was still learning. Jim Bentley had also signed for us and he was a big player of us a strong centre half who later became captain when Stewart Drummond left to join Chester the year after. Lee Colkin had also signed and was a very good left back who was a regular for a couple of seasons before injury and Perks doing so well in that position making it his own, I shared a house with Lee just around from Christie Park. I remember one New years Eve we stayed in and it was snowing so we were thinking that the game might be called off so we went down the club and had a look at the ground it was rock solid so we had one or 2 beers at the club but it hadn't be called off yet so we went back to the house and sure enough the next morning the game was cancelled, a New years eve wasted. We under achieved a little with the squad we had but thought next season could be the year we have a real go at going up.

I was a bit hurt at not playing the amount of games I had wanted to and felt I had something to prove so the next season I was hoping to do enough in pre-season to start the season in the starting 11.

There was now squad numbers introduced and the player's names on the back of shirts which was really exciting, because the conference which was now sponsored by Nationwide had secured a lot of TV coverage and had games being shown live on Sky sports. Our first game live on sky sports was against Dagenham Redbridge away, I was a sub and had come on for the last 30 minutes when we were losing 2-0 we ended up getting a either a draw or pulling one back I remember Wayne scoring with me setting it up, I had a lot of the ball and was trying to make the most of being on television trying different things as we were losing anyway.

I had again come home for the summer and was enjoying a break in Guernsey when the sun out it is a beautiful island with some lovely beaches. It is also perfect for training; I still had a year left on my contract and had a rise in wages half way through last season but I was still not on a good wage compared to the rest of the squad even though I had now clocked up near a hundred appearances, none of us younger players were. At the time it seemed that the local based players were on a lot less than the players being brought in, although it is up to every individual to negotiate a contract and some are better than others at it, so I didn't complain.

We started pre-season on the 1st of July as usual and again we were playing some good stuff against the bigger clubs. I think because we liked to pass the ball around and so did the bigger teams it suited us more sometimes where as in the Conference there were a few direct teams, which we came onstuck against at times. We were getting more solid at the back and with Jim Bentley, Ian Swan and Keith Hill who had a wealth of experience and all three were quality we weren't getting bullied against the more physical sides. We also signed Lee Elam who had a really good season and a good goalkeeper in Craig Mawson. We had an excellent squad with lots of good competition for places even in training the competition was strong, there was still good youth coming through with Danny Carlton looking to break in to the team as well as new signings. I had worked hard in pre-season and I thought I had done enough to start the season but it was clear to me I was going to have to be patient as I wasn't going to be the managers first choice. I was again in and out of the team but the team was being changed frequently with such a strong squad if a player was out of form or injured there was always a player of the same ability to fill in. the only thing is when your not getting a frequent run of games it is hard to find any rhythm in your game and it can work coming off the bench and doing really well which in most cases I did do well when coming off of the bench but it doesn't always work out like that.

CHAPTER 13

IPSWICH AGAIN!

ONE GAME IN PARTICULAR that was probably one of my best moments at Morecambe was against Farnborough Town at their place. We were 1-0 down and needed a win to secure a spot in the conference play-offs. I came on with about 20 minutes to go, the ball was crossed in and I was there to finish with a nice volley, with 5 minutes to go I got the ball inside our own half and ran with it beating 3 players there was a team mate either side of me but I kept going and took on another player before reaching the edge of the box and shooting with my left foot the ball went into the bottom corner and everyone jumped on me. So we were secured a spot in the play-offs. Before this we again had done well in the FA cup we had seen off Chesterfield in the first round where we scored in the last few minutes in a dramatic game. We had scored first with Lee Elam opening the scoring then they equalised and the last 10 minutes Jim brought on me, Perks and Tomo. Me and Perks played a 1-2 then played a ball over the top in which Tomo ran onto to lob the goalkeeper. The second round was against Chester at home where Jim Bentley scored 2 cracking volleys to put us through to the next round the 3rd round of the FA cup the second time in 3 years. Again the excitement was surrounding the town and the prospect of a Premier league side coming to Christie Park or a possible away trip. Amazingly we were again drawn against Ipswich Town this time at there place and they were not in the Premier league but now in the Championship although still a big club there was a crowd of 18,000 at there place. I was playing my part in the cup games but as a sub unfortunately but with the team doing well I was willing to be patient. The build up to the games was again big but was a little different to the last for me as I was starting the previous time and knew I would probably be a sub. We went down to Ipswich the day before the game and went for a light training session at there training ground. It was a brilliant set up there with the pitches in immaculate condition and the indoor dome they have with grass inside and the facilities. We didn't want to leave the training ground that night we were enjoying it that much. My family were coming over again to watch, which wasn't that frequent due to the costs of getting over the only other game my mum had watched that season was against Barnet away.

I was on the bench but nearly always came on although things went pear shaped for my chances of getting on and the teams of winning. After 15 minutes Darren Bent broke free and Jim Bentley had clumsily brought him down for a free kick it was a bookable offence but the referee saw differently and sent him off. Down to 10 men so the manager had to make a tough decision in bringing of a forward player to put on a defender. Then to make matters worse our left back Lee Colkin got injured and couldn't continue so again another defender had to go on for him, Ubey our right back went on at left back and did a good job, so that left 3 forwards still on the bench me, Robbie and Wayne, Rob had just come back from along lay off and he was put on at the end after we were getting beat 3 0. I was gutted not to get on and walked into the changing rooms early to get a shower my mate Vanny had come over to the game also so I got showered and ended up not going on the team bus back to Morecambe but stayed on in Ipswich and went out with the supporters and my mate. It was a good night but a bad journey the next day on the supporter's mini bus back up to Morecambe. Some had to stop and be sick it was a bad journey up the motorway. Back at training on the Monday and were all disappointed with the game and result. Jim Bentley who had scored the goals that had got us into the 3rd round was probably the most gutted with his sending off so early in the game. I was disappointed and not getting on but we all got over it soon enough and it was heads back on to the league, as every footballer said when they get knocked out of a cup competition.

Chapter 14

<u>Runners Up</u>

WE WERE ON A roll again in the league playing some good football in the process. Yeovil town was the top side in our league with us being the second best team, we had out played most of the teams in this league but Yeovil had given us a lesson at home beating us 5-1. They had good players especially in midfield where they were really strong. In the cup at Yeovil we narrowly got beat 2-1 I had come on sub and lobbed the keeper scoring a nice goal to make it 1-1 only for them to score from a set piece in the last minute. Over the season we had been poor away from home but with our home form it still kept us near the top of the league. Farnborough away, the previous couple of games I had been playing but was dropped for this game and was on the bench. If we won this game we knew we would be guaranteed a play-off place with still a couple of games left. We were playing poorly and were losing by a goal with 25 minutes to go, the manager told me to get changed I was going on right midfield. I had been really annoyed about being dropped again, it was driving me mad every time I was in the team it was the same scenario, no matter how I was playing id be brought off after 75 minutes. Then if I didn't play brilliantly I would be dropped to the bench, that was Jim though if you were in the position of a winger or a striker it was odds on that you'd get brought off and it wasn't just me it was anyone playing in that position, Jim is the type of manager who does like to make all 3 substitutions, which is good if you are sub you know you are going to get on but if you are starting you are waiting for that board to come up with your number up sometimes. I came on as sub and with one of my first touches I scored with a volley from close range to draw level then with a few minutes remaining I went on a run from inside our half and shot from the edge of there box with my left foot to score the winning goal, to secure our place in the play-offs. Shelly who had a great season and had scored some important goals himself was suspended for the last 3 games of the season and Jim had told me I would play in my favoured position as a second striker dropping off a front man. We won all 3 games and I was in good form, I had set up a couple of goals and scored a penalty in the final game of the season against Burton Albion. I was excited about the play-offs but I knew the manager would have a tough decision to make whether to bring Shelley back in or stick with me, I expected him to bring Shelly back in but I thought I would play some part in the 2 games. Dagenham and Redbridge was our opponents as we had finished as runners up behind Yeovil who gained automatic promotion to the football league, Dagenham had finished 5th. The first game was away at Dagenham's ground, I was sub, we didn't play that well and we lost 2-1 I didn't come on but I was sure I would come on in the second leg at Christie park. In the second leg we were trailing by 1 goal, it was another really tense game and neither side was playing good football and struggling to break each other down. I was told to warm up to go on 3 or 4 times but we scored and it took the game into extra time. I was itching to get on and thinking that if I got on and scored it could be the goal to take us into the final. The manager decided not to put me on, one of the last kicks of the game Robbie Talbot had a chance to clinch it for us but his shot went wide. So it was penalty kicks to decide who would go through. This was pressure for the lads out there but I still would have wanted to take 1, we had practised penalties during the week a couple of the experienced lads who had played play-offs before at Wembley were having a joke saying how they'd scored there penalties before and that. Both of them missed in the shoot out and we were beaten. After the last kick was taken I was stood next to the manager who said to me I should have put you on to take a penalty, it didn't make any difference afterwards it was a disappointed dressing room afterwards understandably, fair play to Dagenham though who battled the whole game. They got beat by Doncaster in the final at Villa Park.

CHAPTER 15

NEW CONTRACT OFFER

A FEW DAYS LATER I met with Jim as I was out of contract, he told me that I would be offered the same deal as last season. Which wasn't great especially considering the season before and the fact I was full-time? No pay rise after coming second in the league and scoring 8 goals and getting into the 3rd round of the FA Cup, and making 40 appearances. I told Jim that I thought the offer was a joke and that I would weigh up my options in the summer. I went home back to Guernsey and had a long think about what I wanted to do next season, I didn't want to leave at all but at the same time I felt I was being taken advantage of because I wanted to be at the club and I had been there a while and was settled. I wasn't the only player who wasn't happy about what they had been offered and a few had left for the same reason. We were now full-time but I was still on the same wage but Morecambe had said to me that that's all they had to offer me the same deal and I couldn't go anywhere because I was under 24. I said I wasn't excepting their offer. Although I couldn't leave for free there would be a tribunal if I joined another team. There were 3 clubs interested in signing me and they were all conference clubs, Margate, Farnborough and Northwich Victoria. I went down to Farnbrough and spoke with there chairman at the time

Vic Searle, there manager was Tommy Taylor. I liked Vic and had discussed terms with him the only stumbling point was the money that they would have to pay for me. Things weren't getting any better at Morecambe contract wise and I was on the phone to directors from the club trying to sort things out but I was determined to leave the club now and start a fresh challenge. Margate manager Chris Kinnear was also interested and I had spoken with him a couple of times, Terry McFlynn was also there it was far away though and they too were concerned about a fee. I spoke with Northwich Victoria manager Steve Davis and they approached Morecambe about the possibility of signing me, Steve told me that Morecambe wanted to keep me but to keep him informed if anything changed. I went back to Morecambe for pre-season a day or 2 late but quickly got into the training. I was left out in the first couple of friendly matches but was then back involved for the last few, but I didn't have a squad number or any training kit. After the season we had just had, the highest position in the clubs history and reaching the 3rd round of the cup this was how they treat a player. I found out that some of the players who had left in the summer got the same sort of treatment I was getting regarding there contract so they decided to go somewhere else. It was a strange situation especially as I was only asking for an extra 50 pound a week. I was still registered with Morecambe and after being left out of the squad for 1 or 2 games I was now recalled to the squad and made 5 more appearances for them that season before leaving. My last game was against Burton Albion, I had come on as a sub and had played really well setting up the winning goal. After the game Jim and his assistant Andy Mutch pulled me into the office and told me that they had convinced the board of directors to drop the fee they were asking and that they didn't think it was fair to stand in my way if I wanted to move on to further my career but they said that they wanted me to stay and sign a new contract. I thanked them for everything but told them that if there was no change in there offer I didn't feel like I should stay. It was an emotional last game for me as id been there for 5 years and Jim had given me a chance when no-one else did.

CHAPTER 16

NORTHWICH VICTORIA

NORTHWICH WERE REALLY KEEN to sign me and had offered me an extra 400pound a month and it was a part-time club. It seemed the right thing to do join Northwich but after 1 game I regretted the decision but knew I had to stick with my decision. It was a rushed move there as I met with the manager Steve Davis on the Thursday at the holiday inn hotel and he wanted me to sign on for the match on the Saturday against Halifax. I just signed non-contract so I wasn't tied down there and he said if I done well after a couple of games I would get a better deal. Non-contract forms basically meant that I would get paid up until I wanted to move on or the club wanted me to move on. Northwich were really struggling and although we had a lot of good individual players as a team we didn't gel and all the managers coming and going bringing in different players and changing the team every week didn't really help matters. The Halifax game was a nightmare and we lost 4-3, I hardly got a kick on the left wing and was defending the whole time I was on. I was dropped the next game and played a game in the reserves to get a whole game under my belt. It was difficult right from the beginning when Steve got sacked after the next game. Alvin Macdonald became manager from Marine, after 3 or 4 games Alvin was starting to get rid of players on non-contracts so he could bring in some of his own players, he tried to get rid of some contract players to get them on loan but he couldn't. He kept me and Johnny Allen the only players left on non-contract, I travelled in with Johnny as he was from Carlisle and came past Lancaster on the way. He kept us for a couple of months until he released John on the Thursday and myself the week after, he seemed genuinely disappointed to release us both but then again you can never tell with football managers they can be good actors. As I was walking out the door my old team mate Colin Potts was walking in to sign that night he was coming in for me. I did play in a few good games for Northwich, we played Tranmere Rovers at there ground in a cup game in Alvin's first game in charge, I scored and we won the game. We also played really well in the FA Cup against Halifax beating them 1-0, I had a solid game in midfield marking a former team mate Lee Elam. We drew Kidderminster Harriers away in the first round proper in the cup, Jan Molby was in charge of them when they were in league 2. I had a good game especially in the first half although we got beat 2-1. In the match report I read that there manager Jan Molby had told them to get tight to me and that I was causing them problems.

When Alvin released me he was sacked a couple of days later and Shaun Teale took over, there secretary had asked if I wanted to stay to impress the new manager but I had started training at Morecambe with a view to re-signing. I was delighted when Jim had asked me to sign a contract with the club. I was waiting for the director to ring me so I would get everything sorted and sign, the meeting kept getting delayed during that time the manager at Stafford Rangers rang me to go down there I wasn't driving at the time though and it was far plus id agreed to sign with Morecambe. After a week or so after nothing had been sorted Jim pulled me into his office again and told me that he needed a defender bringing in and could afford both of us. I couldn't believe it and I still don't know the real reason behind that decision not that it matters now, I was bitterly disappointed. It was coming up to Christmas and all the lads were going out in Manchester so I went out with them and got a flight back to Guernsey the next day for Christmas and was contemplating staying there for the rest of the season. I had a phone call from Lee Turnbull at Barrow, he wanted me to sign for him up there just turning up for games and do some training at Morecambe. I didn't want to drop down a league at the time and I was still gutted about what had happened at Morecambe.

I got a job with my mate's dad Charlie Archenoul who needed a hand doing some labouring so I was working with him for a few weeks. I also signed on with local side Vale-Rec, I only played 2 games for them as 3 games were cancelled whilst I was over there. They were managed by Ray Blondel and Kevin Le Tissier who were Matt Le Tissiers uncle and brother respectively, who had themselves been top players at local level and many have said were good enough to play in England. They were good guys and the lads I had played with at junior level were still there. I enjoyed the 2 games despite the poor surfaces on the pitches we played on, they were waterlogged with puddles on although we played some good football in those games. I had got my appetite back for football and although the first few days at work were ok, I knew I needed to get back playing football somewhere to make a living.

Chapter 17

Glenavon Irish Premier League

I HAD A LOOK at some contacts I had, I thought id give Jim Harvey a call first to see what he thought. Although I felt Jim had let me down once or twice he had also helped a lot with my football and ive always had a lot of respect for him being a great coach. Jim had told me Glenavon FC had been in touch with him from the Irish premier league, Jim had played for them before masking the move to Arsenal, they were looking for a striker. He had mentioned my name and asked me if I was interested going out there. Why not? I thought. The chairman of Glenavon was Roy Ferguson, he rang me up Roy was very passionate about his club. Tommy Kincaid the newly appointed manager at the club also rang me and they were keen to get me over as they were bottom of the league by a lot of points. That didn't matter to me at the time though as I just wanted to get back in to professional football again. They wanted me to come over right away to negotiate a deal as they didn't want to talk terms over the phone. They paid for my flights to Belfast and sent the tickets over, Glenavon is in Lurgan. When I arrived at the airport they had a driver waiting for me. I was really impressed with the set up there with the stadium was lovely and the pitch was a good surface which was a major plus point. The people there were extremely welcoming. I was more than happy to sign a contract with them I agreed a good deal for me with my accommodation and flights to and from England paid for. I was to stay with a family in Lurgan whilst I was over for the weekends.

The family I was staying with was the club secretary and his wife Angela and Harry who were a lovely couple and they made me feel at home there. In my contract I had written in that I would be flown from Manchester on a Thursday train that night and play a game on the Saturday, after the game fly back to Manchester, everything paid for by the club. My dad was living in Morecambe at the time so I was staying with him during the week. There were 7 or 8 players from the Irish league playing for different teams who were commuting from England, Scotland and southern Ireland. They would all meet up at the airport and have a few beers or magners before the flight home. Nigel Jemson who was at Ballymena was one who was commuting and for us at Glenavon there was Michel Renwick who lived in Scotland and myself. I would see a lot of Michel as we were both full time pros so we would coach on the Thursday and Friday going into primary schools with the community officer Seamus Heath and his son Ben Heath who also played for Glenavon and who I would see a lot. I enjoyed the coaching and living in Ireland so much I decided to stay there full time and not travel back.

My debut game was away to Newry, I hadn't played competitive football for a while and had just one training session with the team before the game. It showed unfortunately as I was well off the pace and had a nightmare and we got beat fairly easily. I was a bit embarrassed after the game, Glenavon was expecting a lot from me and the fans were too, I could sense their disappointment. I rang home and spoke to my mum and dad, I told them I think I'm going to get a flight home I'm not sure ive got it anymore. They said to me to wait a little longer to see how the next game goes and take it from there and if I still feel the same way then get a flight back. I knew I didn't want to go back to grafting for a living so I trained hard that week and prepared for the next game that was at home. I was feeling a lot more confident and was ready for the game, my first few touches of the game were good and then Shane McCabe had a shot from long range which hit the bar and I was the only player to follow the ball and headed the rebound passed the keeper. I went on to have a good game and we won the game, which was the first win for Glenavon in the league for some time so everyone was pleased with the result. I was enjoying the training and was getting to know the lads well. Most of the lads liked a drink so we would be out in Belfast most weekends and id often stay at one of there house on a weekend and go out where they stayed in there home town. Pete Batey, Dave Scullion, Andy Hamilton, Steve Hyndes, Ben Heath and Aiden McVeigh were all local to where I was staying so I went out with them mostly. I enjoyed the coaching a lot after I got used to it but at first that was also difficult as a lot of the kids weren't used to my accent and I therefore had to speak more loudly and slower so they could understand me.

My first month was great and I was playing well I had scored 2 goals and 1 of them was against the top side Linfield at Windsor park in front of 5,000 crowd. We had got beaten but we had enough chances to win the game. I had set up my strike partner Paul Mcknight twice almost identical chances but he missed both. It was always good watching the highlights on the television every Saturday after the game. A home game against Ards I received Glenavon's player of the month, unfortunately I got sent off after 20 minutes. I received a 5 match ban and I was annoyed at myself for reacting to a late challenge. I was tackled from behind and retaliated both of us got our marching orders. As I would miss a lot of games I asked if I could go home for a while. The club was great with me, they paid for my flights and sent my wages over every week. I was gutted though as I would only be eligible to play for the last 2 games of the season and we were now sure to be relegated to the first division. Nothing had gone for us that season and we conceded late goals and penalty kicks for fun. It would be first division football for Glenavon next season which was a disaster for the club considering the size and support of it. I came back for the last 2 games of the season which were against Cliftonville and Portadown. We were already relegated but the club still wanted to finish these games well and Portadown was a derby game so there would be a big crowd on. I played well against a real physical Cliftonville side and we won the game 1-0,

I was glad to finish the game in one piece, they had been a club my dad had supported when he was younger. The last game against Portadown was 2 days later and my legs were really stiff as I hadn't played for a while. Portadown was a good side and Gary Hamilton scored a couple of goals against us.

The fans were brilliant with me the whole time I was at Glenavon and in the last game I will never forget them chanting my name the whole game. I'm extremely grateful for my experience at Glenavon and shall always have fond memories there. The manager Tommy Kincaid had rang me all summer to try and get me to stay and win promotion back up to the premier league and offered me a good deal to go back but I didn't want to drop a division and I wanted to return to England, with which club I wasn't sure yet. Morecambe had said I could go pre-season training with them to get fit so I went there and Barrow wanted me to go up there which was an option. I hadn't anything concrete sorted out yet though but I decided to book into a cheap guesthouse in Morecambe and go training and find a club myself.

Chapter 18

Lancaster City

At the local gym I bumped into Ryan Elderten who I had known a little then, he was playing at Lancaster City after being released by Stockport County. He said I should give Lancaster a call, I spoke with thair manager Phil Wilson who then told me to come down for pre-season training. I was training with Morecambe during the day and with Lancaster at nights. They had just entered the newly formed Nationwide conference north league which was the top ten clubs from the Unibond premier and the top ten clubs from the doctor martins premier to form this league, which is mirrored in the south of England and is called the conference south. Phil offered me quite a good deal and a job working for the chairman, plus they would find me accommodation. It was a house joined on to the Dolly Blue Tavern I had told them that I had agreed to go up to Barrow to talk with them and play a game for them before I made a decision. Lee Turnbell was the manager there and he had wanted to sign me before. I went up to play a game against Scottish side Queen of the South, I had played well and thought I would be negotiating a deal after the game. Barrow have a good fan base and it's a club with a lot of potential. Lee told me he wanted to see me play tomorrow against a local side they play every year to have one more look at me before sorting a deal out. I had really bad blisters after the game and after warming up on the Sunday after a team night out the night before I could hardly walk on them let alone run. If I was to sign I would be turning up only for games and would train with Morecambe during the days as the Barrow players were from the north east and they didn't train together. Lee said he wanted to see me play one more game but I had told him that I wanted something sorted out quick as I had been keeping Lancaster waiting and plus he had seen me play before so I didn't understand the need for one more game.

Lancaster was really keen for me to sign and it was a lot easier for me to get to rather than get a train to Barrow. Also after training with Lancaster for a week or 2 I was starting to get to know the lads and it was a good laugh there. I signed a year deal at Lancaster and started work for the chairman's company gulf environmental and moved into the dolly blue house next to the ground. The landlady was called Lyn who was the bar manager next door and she was really nice and made me feel welcome straight away. My work was easy enough and I was earning good money playing football and working full time. Pre-season went well and I was fit and raring to go. We had a good side, I was playing as a striker along with Peter Thompson who had once got a transfer from Lancaster city to Dutch premier league side NEC Breda. I had met Tomo before when he came to Morecambe for a short spell, Tony Sullivan was also starting up front for the first couple of games before Phil decided to play just 2 up front instead of 3. Tomo was 6 foot 4 and we worked well up front together, I had started the season on fire and was scoring in most games. There were a few former teammates of mine from Morecambe at Lancaster with Jamie Murphy their Ubey and a couple more. With Lancaster being so close to Morecambe both teams have had a lot of ex-players from each club. I had scored 14 goals before getting mumps, they were horrible my face was swollen like a hamsters. To make matters worse when I went to the doctors to see what was wrong with me there was a student there who had to check all of my glands, it was embarrassing. We had a big cup game the week after and Phil wanted me to play only 1 week after I had got mumps. I played the whole game but felt awful at the end of the game and it knocked me for six. I was in bed for weeks and missed a lot of games. Just after I had recovered and not being out for a month I went for a couple of drinks with some of the lads. I was in a bar called Bentleys when I saw a girl at the bar I said to one of the boys that I liked her. So I started talking to her and told her to sit down and have a chat. I was drunk and I don't think Becky was too impressed but I did get her number. I then made sure it was the right number by calling her in the bar whilst we were talking. After a couple of phone calls that weren't answered I saw Becky out in a night-club Toast where I asked why there was no phone call. After a chat and I was sober this time, I said I will call you one more time and if there is no answer then I won't ring again. I texted her a few days later and we went on a date to the cinema and watched Meet the Fockers. The film was so funny I couldn't stop laughing and I was anything but cool. We have been together for nearly three years now.

I was back playing but was on the bench against Alferton. The game was at their place, we were 2-1 down when I came on and scored 2 crackers. I was on the left and cut inside twice to score from outside the box the second nestling right in the top corner. After that game I was back in form with only a small dry patch in front of goal. I ended the season with 2 goals against Runcorn at Southport's stadium my 21st and 22nd league goals of the season taking my tally to 24 for the season. We also enjoyed a good FA cup run getting to the first round and playing Mk Dons at there National Hockey Stadium knocking out conference side Scarborough in the previous game. I was out of contract and hadn't heard anything until after the game I was negotiating my contract with Phil Wilson in the bar at Southport. I was going on holiday to South East Asia the week after with my mate Dan. And I wanted my contract sorted out before I went on holiday for 6 weeks. Phil was very shrewd when it came to contracts and didn't give any thing away. We managed to agree a deal and I had a 200 pound a month pay rise and a signing on fee of £3,500 over 2 years plus my accommodation was free with no bills. I was happy with signing a 2 year deal at the club I have always enjoyed playing for. The only negative thing is the clubs small attendances compared to the rest of the league Lancaster were only getting 3-400 at home being one of the smallest attendances but those who travelled away from home with us were brilliant as well and supporting us all over the country spending a lot of there hard earned cash in the process. I had everything written down by the secretary of the club and everything was sorted my first payment would be going into my account whilst I was away.

When I got back from my 6 weeks travelling around Thailand, Cambodia and Laos I had gone into to see the secretary as I had a letter through the post saying the cheque they had put in had bounced. When I went in he told me that the chairman had resigned, so I had a meeting with the new chairman Steve and the directors. They then told me that they couldn't afford my contract and that Phil had said he hadn't agreed this deal. I rang Phil up with everyone there and he was lying to me on the phone, it was all in writing. They told me the club was in a financial mess and they could only afford my basic wage and £1000 pound signing on fee. I understood that it was difficult times for the club but couldn't understand why Phil didn't tell the truth which he had admitted to me some time after. I said id have to think about things and they were fine about that and they offered me £500 in cash there and then but I said I wouldn't take it unless I was going to stay. I spoke with Stalybridge Celtic manager John Reed and he could match Lancaster's offer but with no accommodation but I decided to sign a year with Lancaster and things were all sorted out a week or so before pre-season training.

CHAPTER 19

WORLD ISLAND GAMES

I WOULD BE BACK late though as I was called up to play for Guernsey in the World island games in the Shetlands up in north Scotland. The island games is a tournament held every 2 years and has islands competing in it such as Bermuda, Greenland, Cayman Islands, Gibraltar, Isle of Man, Western isles and other islands from over the world. Some island had taken a week by boat to get to the Shetlands for the start of the games, events in the games vary from which island is hosting the games. The most popular events include men's and woman's football, cycling, athletics, swimming, basketball although in Shetlands basketball wasn't in it I was disappointed as a lot of my mates play in the Guernsey basketball team. Although Shetlands wasn't the most exotic destination compared to all of the other islands I was looking forward to playing in a tournament and playing a lot of games in a short space of time. I was shocked though when the Guernsey manager had told me it would be £600 to go to the games. There was only so much sponsorship and we had to stay on a cruise ship as all of the hotels had been filled. A rich island like Guernsey surely you shouldn't have to pay that amount of money to represent your island. That's the case though in every tournament and it's the same with the other sports too. I really wanted to go though and see what it was like so I paid the money.

Before I met up with the squad for training I had been told some people weren't happy at my inclusion because I wasn't playing locally in Guernsey and was playing in England I thought that was a bit strange I was born on the island. I went over to Guernsey a few weeks before the tournament to train with the team and I found the first couple of sessions difficult with just coming back from holiday and getting to know how the lads played etc. Once the games started everything was fine though. On the day before we were to fly out to the Shetlands my left arm started to swell up near my elbow. I showed it to my mum and she put some ointment on it and strapped it up. It was a bite from when I was on holiday where I had been bitten badly in Cambodia staying in a beach hut I had left a light on and fell to sleep there was a rat and a lizard on the roof and kept looking to see if they moved on to the floor I didn't have a very good sleep that night. The bite had a really big red circle around my arm most of the bites I did get turned into blisters which swelled up and puss came out leaving a deep hole in my skin.

On the day of the flight it started to swell up big so on the plane I went down to see the doctor he had a look at it and told me I would need antibiotics and to see him when we landed. I was hoping the tablets would sort it out quickly and couldn't believe the timing. We had a game the next day against Orkney. I spoke with the doctor and the manager and there wasn't any improvement in my arm the next day and they ruled me out of the game, Orkney were one of the weaker teams so it made sense to sit this one out although I hate missing games. There was a big game in a days time against Western Isles who were a team that were quite fancied, we beat Orkney in the first game but we were far from convincing against them.

I had been declared fit to play against Western Isles, I had my arm well strapped, this was my debut for the senior Guernsey team as I hadn't represented Guernsey since I was 18 as I was professional at Morecambe and therefore couldn't represent them. It was a quick start to the game and they weren't a bad team they took the lead but we were a better side and it showed when we levelled I scored to make it 1-1 then I made it 2-1 with a back heel I remember running off to celebrate my winning goal only to see a field full of sheep. My blister on my arm had burst during the game and it wasn't a pretty site in the changing rooms after the game, my arm looked horrific. There was puss and blood pouring out of it, it was such a relief that it had burst though because the pressure was unbearable. I had to call the physiotherapist to see me that night as the bacteria had built up again and he was squeezing away at my arm to get all of the puss out about 12am and he had had a couple of drinks too. The doctors and physiotherapists were excellent though and very professional. The antibiotics were making me sick though and I was always going to the toilet and I had lost my appetite. The next game was against Greenland, they had been training together in Denmark for 2 weeks and looked the part. Before the game in the warm up they looked really professional, good on the ball and kitted out in nice Adidas gear with squad numbers I thought we would be in for a game here. We played brilliantly that game and passed the ball around and looked like a good team that day, I was impressed with a lot of our players. I got on the ball a lot and we won 5-0 scoring some excellent goals I set up a couple but didn't get on the score sheet. It was also special to play in a game with my younger cousin who I hadn't played with before. Although I had a good game I was really starting to feel ill from the tablets and not eating. When we weren't playing I was in bed I only joined in with a couple of training sessions. It was raining there as well all the time which wasn't the best especially whilst staying on a cruise ship. We were now through to the final now after winning our group we did have one final game against Ynys Môn who we beat comfortably the manager rested a few of us for the final where we to play against the home team Shetlands. I hadn't eaten properly now for a couple of days and was feeling real weak I was sharing a room with my cousin Darren and Ollie MacKenzie they couldn't believe how much I slept. I do like my sleep at the best of times but this was ridiculous. I wasn't right at all and if it had been a league game I would of never played but with the game being the final of the world island games against the home nation Shetland and in front of 6,000 people I was desperate to play. Rather selfishly I declared my self fit for the game and started up front the atmosphere was great with there being no seats everyone was stood up. I played as long as I could but didn't think it was fair to the team to carry on so after being helped off of the pitch at half time by the physio I told the manager to change things and I came off. We ended up losing to a very average Shetland team and I was so annoyed that I wasn't fully fit as I know we would have had a better chance of beating them. We got a silver medal at the closing ceremony but I didn't stay at the party long as I wasn't feeling great still.

I had a phone call from Lancaster to say we had a friendly against Man United so that cheered me up a bit. Pre-season had started and the lads had just played one friendly against an Emmerdale select team off of the television soap. The next game was against Man United, they were mostly 18, 19 year olds with one or 2 first team squad players Chris Eagles being the main player for them. He scored a cracking goal from the half way line who lobbed our former Man United keeper Ryan Yeamons. Man united team passed the ball around brilliantly and we were chasing shadows the whole game. The first game of the season was away game to Hinkley United in their new stadium which is a lovely set up. We started the game really well and scored from my strike partner Nick Rogan. I was playing well and was feeling sharp until I got tackled late by 2 of the Hinkley players who caught me on the knee. I felt something wasn't right straight away but tried to play on for a few minutes before I went to cross the ball with my left foot and my leg gave way. I was out injured for 5 weeks but in between that time I had tried to play on the injury a few times but it wasn't right. I had been out running with our physiotherapist Liam Enright and I felt fine running in straight lines but as soon as I was twisting and turning it was painful. I rested for a while and waited till it was properly right before returning my first game back was against Hyde United away where we won and I scored 2 goals. I scored 2 more in the next few games, meanwhile off of the pitch the club were still in a lot of financial difficulty and they were trying to cut costs.

The club approached me and told me that they were going to put myself along with the 2 other contracted players on the transfer list. I understood why and I was ok about it if a club came in that I didn't want to go to I didn't have to go so there was no problem.

Les Taylor the commercial director told me he would let me know if anyone enquired about me, the manager wasn't happy about the situation and told me he didn't want me going anywhere. In the first week Lewes came in for me to take me on loan down there in the conference south but the club didn't want me to go on loan and I wasn't going to go that far just on loan.

CHAPTER 20

GAZZAS FIRST SIGNING

MY DAD WAS LIVING with Becky and me at the time and we were at home watching Sky Sports news when Kettering Town came on the television. The new chairman there Imran Ladek had just appointed Paul Gascoigne as first team manager. Gazza was one of my favourite players and I had just read his book, I said to my dad it would be alright if Gazza came in for me, wouldn't it, you never know. A few days later Swanny rang me up he was with Liam the physiotherapist they had found out through the chairman Steve Johnston that Kettering had made an enquiry for me. I thought he was winding me up but he kept on telling me that they had. When I got off of the phone I was buzzing and called some mates and family up to tell them that I might be going down to play for Kettering the team that Gazza is manager of. Then I had another phone call again, it was Swanny "Sorry Zico I made a mistake it was Joe who Kettering came in for, Joe was the other player along with me and Swanny who was on the transfer list, I was gutted and told him that as well". He was apologetic then hung up the phone, next minute a call again and it's Swanny and Liam laughing there heads off, he said "I'm only winding you up they have enquired about you really. I wasn't taking his word for it so I walked around to the secretary's office and asked him about the situation. Kettering had wanted to take me on a 3 month loan and was going to pay Lancaster some money for it. Lancaster wanted to sell me though and I said I would go on loan but would rather go there on a contract if I was to leave here.

The chairman told me he wasn't going to price me out of it but he wanted a reasonable amount for me. I had made it clear to him that it would be too good of an opportunity to miss out on. Phil was not happy about all of this and he told me he didn't want me to go but understood why I wanted to move on. Not long after I left to join Kettering Phil left to join Barrow and Peter Ward took over at Lancaster. We had a game against Northwich who had been relegated the year before due to off the field issues were now top of the Conference north I had been told before the game that Kettering Town officials would be there at the game watching. I played well and scored although we narrowly lost 2-1 with Northwich scoring goals in the 45th and 90th minutes to win the match. I thought there would be a good chance that Kettering would put a bid in for me but new that at least id played well when they were watching and that's all I could do. We had a cup game on the Tuesday and I still hadn't heard anything I played the first half and got injured, my hamstring tightened up when I went to play a cross field pass. It wasn't good timing for me though because on the Thursday night I got a phone call from the chairman Steve Johnston. He told me that they had agreed a fee with Kettering and that they wanted me to go down that same night to have a medical and sign a contract.

I was in town having a coffee when Steve rang and Imran phoned me too, everything was rushed. They also put a little bit of pressure on me by saying that they were looking at signing another player if I couldn't get down. I didn't want to miss out on the opportunity so I told Imran I would be down there tonight, I was texting and ringing Becky who was in a lecture at university and had her phone switched off. I couldn't get through to her and was panicking that she wouldn't get back in time for us to drive down to Kettering. I rang Imran and explained to him that I'd be late and would miss training, I didn't want to train anyway as my hamstring wasn't right still. And I didn't want to tell them that I was injured in case that put them off. I asked the secretary at Lancaster to print me off a map to get down there and directions. It would take 3 hours to get there. On the way down I was talking with Becky about what sort of contract I was going to ask for but I wasn't sure what sort of money Kettering were paying but I definitely wanted a full time contract. I also knew that I was going to have to move down to Kettering because it was so far away. The club were still part time but the club were on the verge of going full-time and were preparing for this. Imran had told me on the phone that the club would put Becky and I up in a hotel after training. We arrived down to the ground at 8.30pm the lads were still out training I met with Imran and one of the directors.

After a long chat and Imran selling the club to me we got down to talking about money, they asked me what I wanted and I told them that I wanted £20,000 a year if we stay part time and £25,000 a year when we go full-time. He told me that we would be full-time with in a month and the players who had jobs were organising to leave them or try and work around them. I agreed a 2and a half year contract and was really pleased to have signed, I thought the deal was good until a few weeks later the club had signed Anthony Elding for a reported £40,000 and he was getting more than double I was on, I was kicking myself I should of asked for more but I was too busy thinking what Gazza would be like. Eldo was a good player though but it was obvious he wouldn't be staying long at Kettering. Paul Davis was Gazza's assistant and was highly regarded as a coach and from the few sessions he took whilst I was there I could see why. I had to have a medical before I signed and I was dreading it because of my hamstring, it was sore but I managed to get through it ok.

As I was going through my medical the lads were starting to walk in from training and Gazza came into the physio's room gave me a kiss on the cheek and said welcome to new kids on the block. The whole night was quiet surreal and although Kettering was a team in the same league as what I was playing. Things were happening to the club and it was the place to be, all the papers and sky cameras were down at the club constantly and we were warned not to give interviews.

The lads were all tucking into pizzas after training, which was a customary thing after a Thursday night's session. I had recognised Junior MacDougald from playing against him when he was with Dagenham. I went into the manager's room to have a chat with him and Paul Davis and they made it clear that they wanted promotion this season. They wanted me to be part of it and they hadn't been scoring many goals and had a couple of strikers out injured. After a while I got my training kit and left to go back to the hotel, I was in the squad for Saturday. Becky and I drove down to the 5 star spa hotel where we ordered some champagne and a meal. This was the chance id been waiting for the past 2 seasons and everything seemed right at Kettering to progress with them. I rang some friends and family to tell them I had signed and my mate told me it's about time you got a decent move. The next morning we had a sauna and a steam then drove back up to Lancaster, it was a long drive although it was a straight forward run up the motorway. When we got back up I went to the garage and brought a Renault Clio. On the Saturday I met with my new team mates at a hotel near Liverpool for a pre-match meal before the away match against Vauxhall Motors. We had a pre-match meal before every away match and I usually met up with Wayne Diuk and Jamie Patterson who also lived a fair distance from Kettering. Hugh Macauly joined after Gazza left and he was the other player who travelled. I've never really been fond of the pre-match meals when there's not a long distance to drive but with Kettering being the furthest team away in this league I suppose it made sense. The management talked everything through before the game with Paul Davis doing most of the talking and organising, and the manager saying a few bits after him. I thought the club was very professional was my first impressions. I was named on the bench and I was kind of hoping not to play at all with my hamstring not being right still but I though adrenaline would get me throught if I did. Vauxhalls crowds are always small but Kettering had brought a good following and were vocal through out the game and they gave me a good reception when I came on with the score being 1-1, I played the last 20 minutes and done o.k. but the management were far from happy after the game and we were in the changing rooms for ages before getting showered and changed. We played great football with the ball being passed around the back and through midfield but we didn't create many chances. I was limping when I got back from the game and iced it straight away when I got in but didn't want Kettering to know I was struggling. I was still staying at the dolly blue which Lancaster were still paying for but I was back and forth from Becky's house and digs down at Kettering when I was down there. The next game was on the Tuesday against Redditch at there ground. I drove down the m6 to meet the lads at Corley services where I left my car, we had a pre-match meal and the team was named I was sub. The first half was terrible and we were 3-0 down, I came on at half time but didn't play well at all although we did manage to get a couple of goals back to make it 3-2. Before I went on at half time the manager had told me that I would be starting in the cup game on Saturday. After the game it was about 11pm before we got back on to the coach and I had to drive back up to Lancaster yet. Corley was about an hour away from Redditch after getting on to the coach and leaving the car park the bus broke down. They had to call another coach out from Kettering; it was going to be a long night. It could have been even longer if the Redditch secretary hadn't come past and offer me a lift back to Corley services. I went on the bus to let the management know I was getting a lift and left. After getting dropped off I arrived back at Becky's at 3am, Kevin Dixon had signed that night from a local team in Newcastle, he had played for Leeds and Barnsley before joining his local team and had known Gazza for a while. Kev was a centre midfield player. We were staying in the same digs in Kettering, after playing in a midweek reserve game against Stafford which I also played in Kev signed a 2 year deal but left after Gazza had gone because he was getting messed around with his deal. After the game I again felt that my hamstring wasn't right and missed training on the Thursday to get some treatment. On the Saturday we played Farsley Celtic in the cup but I wasn't fit to play but still went on the bench in case of an emergency. Over the next week or so I stayed down at the George hotel which the club had been paying for us. It wasn't a bad hotel and all our food was paid for I stayed there for about a month, Kev was also there for a couple of weeks. We also got free use of the local gym La fitness where we went during the day. On the Tuesday all the first team and reserves trained, I could sense in training that the coach Paul Davis was being a bit funny with me and that was made clear when he read out the whole first team squad apart from me to do some drills. That really annoyed me but I just got on with training, I knew something was going on though and I was starting to wonder who it was who actually wanted me there, there was tension between Gazza and the chairman. Some of the stuff that was said and what was going on was comical for a football club, Jamie Patterson who Gazza had made club captain when he came had released him and Christian Moore had been placed on the transfer list, there was a bit of unrest in the squad. Things definitely weren't right between the chairman and manager, tension was building between the pair and the manager had mentioned the chairman a couple of times. The next week and Gazzas last week in charge was a strange and sad week as well. George Best had passed away. I remember watching videos of the legend with my dad mostly on a Saturday night when he would come home after some beers and id make him a cup of tea and it was either the George Best video, The Boys from Brazil or Jinkie Johnston from Celtic. Gazza was upset understandably on the day of George Bests funeral and it must have been hard with us having a game on the same day. Before the game it was easy to see that there was a strain on his face and it was the one and only time that I seen him have a drink., but you could hardly blame him that day for having a drink before the game. In the team talk before the match he just said to go out there and win the game for his pal George. Unfortunately we didn't play that well but managed a draw. I didn't play in that game as I was still injured. The club had paid reportedly £10,000 for me from Lancaster and it hadn't been a great start for me with this niggling injury I hadn't really trained a lot. But I knew that in a few weeks when I was fully fit I would be playing and learning a lot from the management there. Before that week Gazza had been on at me to move down and commit so I had looked around a few houses and flats to rent.

Early on in the next week we were called in for an emergency meeting down at the club, Gazza had been sacked as manager of Kettering Town, I had heard it on the radio in my car on the way down and we were all wondering what's going to happen now, I was gutted when I heard. He was the reason I had signed in the first place and I had committed to a long term contract. When I arrived all of the lads were in the changing room, waiting to find out what was happening and then the next thing Kevin Wilson walked in to the changing rooms. I've taken over as manager as from today and have signed a 3 year contract. You all know what I'm about and how I work, well most of you anyway. There was four of us left who Gazza had brought in Kev, Michel Mackezie who had been at Kettering before but had been released by Kevin Wilson when he was manager the previous time he was in charge, which was unlucky for Michel, and Jordan Fowler who I had got to know quiet well and was a good lad, Jordan had been at Arsenal all through his youth and was a pro there he worked with Paul Davis at the club where he was a coach. Jordan's first game was the same day as Gazza and Paul Davis left and he too had signed a long deal. But he left after a couple of months because Kev didn't play him. The players that Gazza had brought in were obviously disappointed that he had gone but not everyone was sad to see him go. Especially when Kev had come back because this was his squad before Gazza had taken over. After training I went into the bar at the club to have a chat with Imran, he was busy though having a live slagging match with Paul Gascoigne live on Sky Sports I was watching Imran and then later Kev Wilson talk live on sky sports news it was crazy! I was just watching it all while sipping on a coke.

Right the circus is over now, I don't care what happened whilst I was away, and all this playing out from the back and fancy football stops now. We are going to become hard to beat again and start grinding out some results and climb the league. My first impression was I cant see me fitting in with this guy. The one connection we did have was that we had both played for Northern Ireland and Kev had won many caps for them too especially whilst he was at Chelsea, any hope of that connection going for me quickly fizzled out as after one game as an un used sub he shoved me in the reserves and I was convinced he was going to leave me there to rot for the remainder of my 2 year contract.

The one thing that I will remember the most from Gazzas reign and as my boss was a time before a game a week after I had joined.

Before he was giving his team talk before kick off we were outside the changing rooms together and he said to me I'm no longer Gazza the football legend, well ill always be that but I'm your gaffer, the boss, that's all. Believe in yourself and every time you go on to the pitch believe that you are the best player on the pitch have that in your head every game you play in even if you aren't the best believe that you are. When I was playing I thought I was better than Pele, Best, Maradona, I probably wasn't but I honestly believed I was when I was on the pitch. I will always remember that, I was just stood there taking everything in like a 15yearold schoolboy.

Kevin Wilson also stated that there would be none of this full-time nonsense we are a part time club and we will remain that way unless we get promotion and then it might be a possibility. I then thought about my contract and thinking it would only be a month until my money would go up but now if were not going full time ill be on that lower wage. I had a chat with Kevin after that first night when he arrived as he spoke with everyone. He told me he hadn't seen a lot of me but thought that my best position was as a 3man forward line. He didn't play with 3 forwards and didn't like to, in the next couple of weeks he made it clear to me that I wasn't in his plans long term but possibly short term I would be, that would be a problem as I had another 2 years on my contract left. In fairness to Kev he always told me to my face what he thought and you can't ask for much more than that even if it was negative things said, I wish more managers would do the same instead of just telling you what you want to hear. The next couple of weeks I was getting down about football and with not playing my confidence was low and I lost interest in training. I was doing a lot of travelling to training and was staying in digs in Kettering less and less, now I had to pay for my digs when I stopped over. I spoke to Imran and told him I wasn't happy about the situation. Imran had asked me to go down training with MK Dons and was asking me to move down to Kettering. After a week or so I agreed to go down training but didn't want to commit to moving down until I started playing regularly. That week Kev Dixan left as he was getting messed about and Jordan was thinking of leaving whilst Michel Mackenzie wasn't getting a look in either but he had been down training with Mk Dons for a while. I had spoke to Jordan about the Dons training and he didn't fancy it either it was a long way to go just to train and I would be paying a lot of money in accommodation and even if we did train it wouldn't mean we would get a game at Kettering. When Kev first took charge again he got a couple of good results but then things went wrong and the team went on a bad run. Kev was manager for a season before Gazza had taken over and when he did take over Imran had asked Kev to move upstairs as Director of Football which he accepted at first but then left after a week or 2. It was obvious that Kev was still a little bitter over the Gazza saga and every excuse he had he would blame Imran and the club for changing things around. I didn't like Kevs methods as a manager and I can't say I enjoyed that spell of playing under him or not playing under him. But after a time I did like him and when he finally gave me chance I think we got on better and had a mutual respect. Whilst I was playing at Lancaster City I had booked a holiday to Alicante for a few days with Becky, I was going to cancel it when I joined Kettering but I didn't get round to it and because I hadn't played we went anyway and I pulled a sickie from training. When we got back into Lancaster my 2 mates Dan and Vanny were at the house and were staying for Christmas. We had a game at Hinkley over the festive period and it was a real long drive Vanny came with me, I had rung the manager to ask him if I needed to travel, his reply was of course you do. So I drove down and got there 5 minutes late, the squad had been named and surprise I wasn't in involved. I joined in with the warm up and done some extra running to keep ticking over. We lost the game and I went to speak with the manager after the game having missed most of the game to go to subway with Vanny in the town centre. I asked him why he wasn't giving me a chance and I told him ill leave if he wants but I want paying up, he said no chance and I asked if I could go on loan, he didn't want me to do that either. I was getting sick of the driving and had a plan that if I could go on loan somewhere up north I would get the same money maybe Kettering pay half and my loan club pay the rest and I wouldn't have to pay all this petrol. I left the ground and drove back getting lost in the process and ending up in Sheffield, at the services I rang Phil Wilson who was at Barrow. He said if I could get away for free then he would give me a good deal to go up there, I said Kev would let me leave for free definitely he told me that after the Hinkley game. When I spoke to Kev a few days later on the phone he told me that the chairman wouldn't let me go for free when he paid that money for me.   I thought they will eventually let me go if im not playing but then again I was thinking that if I could stick it out I might be able to make a few quid but I couldn't do it not playing regularly and I knew I wouldn't. The game after was at home and I couldn't bear travelling down just to watch another game so I rang Kev up and told him I was ill. Kev said to me ill have to get a doctors note for the chairman and he said if I want to be considered for the team then ill have to move down. After Christmas at a training session the assistant manager Tomo who was always supportive towards me had said to me to if you do well in the reserves ill be pushing for you to get a chance in the first team, he said we need something different in the team now and im coming down to the reserve game against Alferton tomorrow night. Anthony Elding had joined us from Stevenage Borough and was also playing in the reserve match. I had a good game and scored, after the game Tomo had come into the changing room and and told me he was impressed and was going to have a word with the manager and it would be up to him to make the decision.

My old team Lancaster City was the next game on the Saturday, Kev pulled me into the office before the game to have a chat with me and told me that I would be starting today on the right hand side of midfield he said id worked hard and had deserved a chance in the team. I scored a goal in the first half with a good strike from long distance that flew in to the bottom corner in off of the post. I did celebrate the goal much to the annoyance of my old team mates who let me know after the game but with all of the frustration I had for the month before it was a relief to score a goal although it was unfortunate that in the game where I get my first goal it happened to be against Lancaster City. Yes I did celebrate but I definitely didn't kiss the badge on my shirt like a couple of the lads had said and it was written in the local newspaper in Lancaster. That's one thing that I wouldn't do unless id been with a club for years and years. We beat Lancaster 2-1 and I went on to play in the next few games and was playing ok, and was starting to earn some respect from the manager and the players to some extent as well because I hadn't played any games with apart from a handful of substitute appearances whilst Gazza was in charge. I was sub for the Hyde game which was away for tactical reasons he didn't start with any wingers and that's where I had been playing. We played terribly and were 3-0 down when I came on, I tried to get on the ball and had a couple of long range shots. The manager was fuming after the game but said Zico you done well when you came on, that was the first bit of praise I had received since I arrived at the club. Kev was sacked after the game, I was getting some treatment on the Tuesday and Kev came in to sort his stuff out with the chairman, he walked in to the treatment room to say bye and he said to me that his opinion had changed about me and he was impressed by how I had conducted myself and how I played. He wished me luck and I did the same.

Next up on the Kettering Town FC merry go round was one Morrell Mason to take the poppies hot seat. Morrell came to the club on the Tuesday night initially as the reserve team manager, there was a reserve game on but most of the first team played in it, I scored 2 and had a decent game. After the game he said to me that he expected more from me, and that I was cruising through the game. I thought that was a bit much for his first game in charge as reserve team coach, but there was a lot more from where that came from big Morrell. All the lads were saying who is this man, he appeared from nowhere and was very confident. We couldn't believe what was happening at the club and I was just thinking it was all crazy. There was Imran in his late 20s hiring and firing managers like there's no tomorrow in his first few months as chairman. Imran had come out and told us that he was going to take his time in appointing the next manager and wasn't going to make a rash decision like reappointing Kevin Wilson. Morrell had been manager of Buckingham Town in a league roughly 3 or 4 divisions down from the North conference, but had claimed once during a training session at 10 30 am on a school pitch which was full of stones and the odd bit of glass that whilst in Africa doing some coaching he was at a match where he was invited on to the middle of the pitch before the game in front of 70,000 people to accept a standing ovation. Im not having it myself but he was a likeable person although he done my head right in at times and hed probably say the same thing about me.

On the Saturday we were up against Northwich Victoria who were in great form, Morrell had been named caretaker manager apparently he had been a friend of the chairman's for a while. I was starting on the left wing which is where he played me most of the time and I didn't mind as long as I was playing it didn't matter what position. We won 3-0 and I set Eldo up twice for almost identical goals. It was the perfect start for Morrell, Imran likes attacking football and he did to be fair to him. He had brought in Dan Nicholls as a coach and Imran told me I would play a lot more under Morrell than Kevin Wilson, also brought in was Alan Biley who had been Kevin Wilson's assistant manager the previous time he had been in charge. Our training sessions were moved from the ground to Milton Keynes training ground which was even further away for me, where we trained in the dome indoors. Morrell wasn't every player's cup of tea and a few of the more experienced players had left. We had won a few games and were playing better and Morrell got the job until the end of the season. Morrell was bringing a lot of players in and was signing them on full time contracts, we were to train with Milton Keynes for a while before we would train together. I went down to Milton Keyenes for training one morning and I had set off at 6am to get there. When I got down to the training ground there was no MK dons players there it was just the 6 of us Kettering players. We hadn't been told training was off and half an hour later Morrell turned up only to run us for an hour, I was well pleased. Morrell had just signed Finish striker Patrik Peter who didn't really play and struggled to adapt to playing and training. After that training for the full timers changed back to training in Kettering at some local school there and then changed to another place a little better than the school pitch. We now had about 8 full time players and we would train with the youth team during the day and then with the rest of the lads at nights twice weekly. After the first week of training full time I received my wage slip only to see that my wages hadn't been increased, so I didn't turn up for training the next day and when Morrell rang I told him the reason why. The week after everything had been sorted and I had my increase in wages by £100. After tax it worked out at £15 I was gutted I would be better off staying part time and I mentioned that but I didn't go part time. Morrell had sent out letters to all of the part time players demanding that they do extra 1 day week training during the day if they can get off work.

My sister had a flat in Birmingham so I was staying there during the week and then going back up to Lancaster on weekends to see Becky. My car broke down one day on the way to training we got to Stafford before we stopped at services. I rang the manager and chairman to let them know I wouldn't make training in Milton Keynes, I did manage to drive the car down to my sisters, the hazard lights were on and I was driving really slow. There was a man who worked for AA at Stafford services, I asked him to help us but when I said I wasn't with AA he stopped and said there's nothing he can do. I got fined by the club £100 for missing training and I had to pay further few hundred to get the car fixed.

Every Wednesday Morrell had us in the gym at LA Fitness for a spinning session on the bikes for 75 minutes, which was really hard but good training. After our spinning session we had to go into a room for a cool down, we were there lying on the floor 8 of us in a circle holding hands with our eyes shut and Morrell was talking words of wisdom.

We had a massive squad and the team was changed nearly every game no matter what the result was, sometimes we would play brilliantly and win comfortably then the next game the team was changed. I played a lot of games in a 3 man midfield for Morrell and I enjoyed it mostly. I scoreol 4 in total for Kettering and 8 for the season. I was still in and out of the team though and on at least 2 occasions I had played well and we had won I wouldn't even be in the squad for the game after. One time during training Morrell was chatting to us all and told us what he thought of us individually and he told me I hadn't been doing enough in games. I said fair enough but I have been playing out of position, why don't you play me in the position that I was signed for, as a striker. I had scored 27 goals for Lancaster in just over a season in the same league, I had been at Kettering 4 months now and I still hadn't played in the position

I came for. I had played left midfield/wing, right midfield/wing, centre midfield and once or twice as a full back. He said ok then you're playing up front tomorrow against Stafford, put your money where your mouth is, no problem I said. Stafford went up that year as well, they were a strong side but so were we and we beat them 2-0 I had a good game and scored from the edge of the box. I played as a striker again the next game at home where we won the game and I was dropped after that game. I didn't play up front again after them 2 games and I was back playing in midfield when I played. We played Nuneaton Borough at home one game and beat them 4-0 I played in midfield and was having a steady game without being brilliant but we scored 2 early goals. At half time Morrell started ripping into me, id had enough of him and started giving him some verbal's back I said if you're not happy then change it. We were on a good roll and were now a bit more consistent but not as much as we should have been with the group of players we had. We missed out on the play-offs that year by a point, our last away game was against Gainsborough away and we still thought we could make the play-offs. I scored after 10 minutes and we won the game but that wasn't enough as the teams above us won as well. The last game of the season was at home and I wasn't even going to be on the bench before one of the lads got injured in the warm up. I couldn't understand his methods at all, after the game he told us all to report for training the week after, the season was now finished but there was one more reserve game and he wanted everyone at the game also there was a letter for the presentation night 2 weeks later and the letter said every player must attend, if you cant attend then see the manager immediately. I went into see him and explained to Morrell that I had booked my holiday months ago and it was a few weeks after the season had finished. He told me to cancel the 2 and a half week holiday so I could go to the presentation evening. If I don't cancel my holiday then ill be fined 2 weeks wages, that was a final straw for me at Kettering and I didn't feel that I could play another season under him. I told the chairman that I wanted to leave; he said there is no way that I am going to let you leave for free. I was now determined to leave although I had 2 years left, I tried to work a pay out with him but he wasn't interested in that. Because he didn't want me to leave Imran told me he wasn't going to pay me to leave. Ive known a lot of players who have been on contracts but the clubs have wanted to get rid of them and the player could make a lot of money getting a pay off, I was thinking I could make a few grand out of this situation but because the chairman didn't want me to go made this doubtful. In the end I just took what I could get and that was only 2 months pay but I only ended up getting a months pay. It makes sense if a player isn't going to feature in the managers plans but has time left on his contract to come to a financial agreement, it saves the club money in the long run and of course the player benefits with a lump sum and then can get another club.

I rang Imran from the Trafford centre where I was getting some clothes for my holiday and I wanted to sort things out before I went. I told him that I definitely wanted to leave and my mind was made up, he said that if I was sure I didn't want to stay then he wouldn't stand in my way. I said that's good but I did have 2 years left and I wanted a bit of money to leave as it was the summer and if I left now I wouldn't get paid during the summer but it was better to agree a deal rather than wait till July, I should of waited really. I received a fax off of the club to sign and it said that I would receive 2 months payment in 2 instalments but on one condition and that is if I should sign for Lancaster City I would not receive any money. I agreed and signed the agreement thinking that I would be signing for Barrow anyway as I had been talking to Phil Wilson a few times, I knew a lot of the lads playing up there and it was a big non-league club.

CHAPTER 21

BACK TO THE GIANT AXE

IMRAN DIDN'T WANT ME re-signing for Lancaster City because he had paid a fee for me. Although I thought I would be signing for Barrow, Lancaster was another option for me and they offered me a really good deal. They had offered me a good weekly salary plus a house with all the bills paid for. I went on holiday and then when I came back Lancaster had called for me to go there and meet them.

Big things were supposedly happening to the club, there was a new ownership taking over with a new chairman, the owner taking over was a millionaire business man who had made his money from father who had businesses in china. When I went down to the club, he wouldn't meet me for some strange reason and I had to be sneaked in to the kitchen with out anyone seeing me in the bar. I met Lyne outside and walked into the kitchen of the dolly blue tavern, I waited in there until the chairman walked in. The chairman came in he was called Charlie, he was dressed in jeans, a baseball cap and t shirt, Charlie started selling the club to me straight away in a strong Irish accent. Everything he said was well over the top regarding the future of the club and it was all really far fetched although I wanted to believe what he was saying because it would be great if it all was true. A lot of people have said the chairman was a gypsy but I didn't think he was. He told me that the first team would all be full time, I was well happy about that, especially with me not having to travel for training and we would be looking to get promoted this season, promotion from the conference into the football league and he was talking about premier league football and pushing for European football bloody hell a bit of forward optimistic thinking is great but one step at a time European football I couldn't keep a straight face.

He said how all our sponsorship and money was coming from China and the silent business man would be made money by Lancaster signing a couple of players from China and then selling the Chinese players shirts with their names on the back in China.

Every player in the first team squad will be on £500 a week and every player will have a shogun car which will be imported over as the silent mans businessman's father had a shogun garage in China.

Charlie seemed to be sucked in by all of this and I don't mind admitting I was extremely hopeful of this happening but was still sceptical and doubtful like others were.

After Charlie had finished talking the manager came into the kitchen to speak with me Gary had been assistant manager the season before and they made him manager, as he started talking to me we both just started laughing he had told me he had been speaking with these people a few weeks now and said he wasn't sure about the whole thing and after weeks of talking with them he said he may as well give it a try and we both didn't have anything to lose by it.

Iain Swan was the other player they had spoke in to about going full time and my mate Liam, and told them the exact same thing that they told me. I told Lancaster I was talking to Phil Wilson but Phil had dropped his contract offer considerably and wasn't offering a signing on fee with less wages than he offered me whilst I was at Kettering, I thought I'm not going to Barrow with that offer especially when he had offered me such a better deal before.

I told him Lancaster want to sign me and were offering a good deal that I couldn't turn down he said Lancaster is in ruins financially and that they owed everybody a lot of money and the people taking over were Gypsies. Meanwhile Gary rang me from Lancaster to tell me that the multi millionaire businessman was a hoax and had been lying the whole time, and he was actually a door to door salesman and delivered newspapers. Swanny had said that he thought he recognised him because he delivered to his house. So, no Showgun I was looking forward to driving that. Gary then went on to say that the chairman was still taking over the club along with another man Chris who were both taxi drivers before taking over Lancaster. They both seemed to mean well but they had obviously taken on a lot more than they expected and didn't really have an idea about running a football club they just loved football I think and thought it would be good to run a club. When they took over lots of people who had followed Lancaster and the directors of the club resigned.

Living at the club it was entertainment all the time with things that were happening there but I didn't get involved in stuff off of the pitch although it was hard not to get dragged into things because I was there all the time. Gary still offered me a good deal to sign part-time and the club started paying me from July rather than the second week of the season as is the normal time semi pro teams get paid from, I agreed and signed a contract and the deal included the house and no bills. When I signed I did say to the club that it was on the condition they don't make the signing official until I had got my final months payment from Kettering. I had received my first payment off of Kettering more than a week late and that was after ringing them up over ten times. My last payment was due and I was constantly ringing the club and trying to ring Imran but he wouldn't answer his phone to me so I kept ringing it was stressful. I had told everyone at Lancaster to keep it quiet about me signing until I got that money but somehow Imran must have found out. Thinking about it now I should have been cleverer about it and made sure I got the money before signing anything but i wanted to get things sorted out for the season. Two weeks after I was supposed to get that payment there was a photo shoot in the local paper to model the kit and it was during the week so no one else could do it so I ended up doing it. There was no way of getting that £1600 now.

The manager had made some good signings in the summer and the budget for the team was probably the biggest in the clubs history, it was certainly much larger than the previous time I was at the club, and really we could of been full time on the wages we were on. The crowds were still low though and it would take a really good run in the league and cups to get the fans back through the gates which the chairman was thinking was going to happen. The pre-season friendlies were all organised in the space of a week as the take over of the club took most of the summer to happen.

Our first league game of the season was against Alferton Town away, I scored early on in the game and we had plenty of chances to win the game but ended up getting beat 2-1. It was like that the first few games we would be the better team but weren't putting away our chances and we were missing open goals and everything, it was frustrating but things would surely have turned around as we had the quality in the team to do so. One of our strikers Ben Jones was extremely unlucky in front of goal and even though his all round game was good he was getting no luck scoring.

Id been getting paid weekly from July along with the rest of the contract players and the non-contract players were getting paid from the start of the season. After a month or so of getting paid we were starting to get messed about with our wages. We went from getting paid every Saturday after the games to getting our wages on a Tuesday after training, apparently it was better for the club because they could sort the finances out from the weekends game and bar taking from the dolly blue. After a couple of Tuesdays getting our wages with out hassle. I was asked to wait until Thursday for my wage. I didn't mind as I was living at the club and I thought it would be a one off. This started happening on a regular basis, I was getting some of my wage on a Tuesday some on a Thursday and the rest on Saturday. I got my wages eventually it was in drips and drabs but I didn't mind as long as I was getting it. This was now happening with all of the lads and some of them were travelling from Bradford and most were from Liverpool. We would finish training on Tuesdays and the lads would sometimes be waiting for an hour or 2 to collect their wage and one time only half of the lads got there wage and the rest had to wait for it. Alarm bells were starting to ring and the lads were starting to wonder what the hell was going on at the club.

On one Tuesday night we got paid by cheque, on the Saturday at the game everyone was asking each other whether theirs had cleared, no-ones had cleared they were bouncing all the way. We had a meeting with the chairman and he told us that it was all a plan to get his partner Chris out of the club by the cheques bouncing. I don't know whether it was true or not but I certainly couldn't see the logic in the idea.

The team was playing through all of this stuff off the pitch, but things were getting heated and some of the lads were already thinking that the club going bust. It was crossing my mind too, how were the club going to pay our wages for the whole season when they were struggling to pay us at the start of it.

I had a call from the manager one night asking me if I would take a pay cut, he had rang most of the squad and one or two had agreed to it. With my football wage being my only source of income I said I couldn't at this moment in time. Next pay day we got our wages and some of the lads had been deducted money from their wage, when they asked the chairman what was going on he told them the manager had told him that they agreed to it.

I didn't really know what was true or not but I was starting to worry what was happening. Chris the commercial manager and director had left the club along with most of the directors. We were as unlucky on the pitch as we were off it but things really came to a head when we had yet another emergency meeting with the chairman. We must have had nearly ten meetings now in the space of a couple of months, it was a joke. Amongst things we hadn't been given any training kit or tracksuit that we were promised in pre-season. The club had apparently agreed a five-figure deal with a sports company. We had home and away kits new but nothing else, we looked like a pub team at training and travelled to our home and away games in shirt and tie. Most people behind the scenes at the club had quit because they wouldn't work with the chairman so with our low home gates of 300 and our high wage bill the chairman was finding it hard to pay us. Now things had got that bad that players that had to travel in were ringing up before training to check whether there money was here and if not they wouldn't come training. I didn't blame them because they were spending money on petrol to get there so if they weren't getting paid they weren't going to drive in for free, you wouldn't go to work for free.

Every meeting we had it was just full of promises and some promises I'm sure the chairman meant but there was no way of him being able to keep them it was just so unrealistic and delusional. He was talking about undersoil heating for the pitch and building a gym and hotel on the ground and renting the car park out to the public, he had so many ideas it was impossible to do them all. Meanwhile the club was living week to week and at any time it could of folded, we weren't sure from each week if we would get paid or have to look for another club, and we were told that by the chairman. The lads had put up with a lot and when we didn't receive the money for the cheque that bounced, then when we didn't get paid that week before an FA Cup game against Scarborough away in the last qualifying round before the First round proper we called a meeting. Some of the older players along with the manager went in to see the chairman. We had all spoke before the meeting as a team, and we had all agreed that if we didn't get the money that was owed to us, we weren't going to turn up. We had agreed to stick together, this game was a big game for the club and there was a bit of money riding on the game. After the meeting the manager came out and said that he was seeing things through no matter what team he had to put out and it was up to us what we were going to do but we had more chance of getting paid if we played than if we didn't. The older players came out and said that they were disappointed in what was said and they were told that there was no guarantee of us getting paid. I was in a difficult situation because I had got on well with Charlie and I was living at the Dolly Blue. I told him that if all of the lads decided that we weren't going to play then I wasn't going to play either. He wasn't happy at all but could understand why I couldn't play if all of the other lads weren't. The next night I had a phone call off of some of the players who told me that most had decided to play the game because there was more chance of us getting paid. It made things a lot easier for me although it was a strange feeling going to the game on the bus and not knowing who was going to turn up. There was about 4 players who didn't turn up because they didn't want to get cup tied if they left. I was happy to stay at Lancaster as long as I was getting paid even if it was in drips and drabs, it was easy for me there with no travelling and I had no out goings with living in the house everything was paid for apart from food. I wasn't sure how things would last though. We had a reserve team who were made up of the best local players from around the local leagues and Charlie was planning to play them all with 3 or 4 of us first team players. That would get rid of the high budget. We went to Scarborough for the game and got a draw which was a great result considering the circumstance. I played centre midfield in an end to end game on a hot day. After the game we stopped off on the long trip back for a beer which was paid for by the chairman. The replay was on Tuesday and the players that were missing on Saturday played we got paid a weeks wage after the game. We got beat that night and a lot of players left after the game and the next game was a completely different team. Most of the team was made up of reserves with 3 or 4 first team players, we played against Hyde and got beat 4-3 in which I played one of my best games that season and scored a quickly taken free-kick from near the half way line. A couple of days after the game the chairman came to see me to tell me that Hyde had put a bid in for me in which he turned down. He told me he was sorting the club out and with the budget being slashed he would be able to pay me every week. Hyde are a good club with a nice pitch but I was under contract and plus with the deal I was on I knew they wouldn't be able to match with my accommodation and wage. Also Barrow was my back up plan as they had been on the phone again and Phil was monitoring the situation at Lancaster. After the Hyde game we had training on the Thursday when I arrived the manager wasn't changed for training as usual and the lads were stood near the stand. When everyone had turned up Gary then told us that he was resigning tonight and was going in to tell the chairman. He was still owed money like the rest of us and said he had had enough. Earlier that day i was on teletext looking on news in briefs and it said that Southport have just appointed former Lancaster City boss as their assistant manager. I was laughing and I rang him up to find out what was happening, he said he hadn't agreed anything yet but I knew he didn't want to tell me he had signed for them. That night we were due some wages but were told we would get them on Saturday. Bails our centre half grabbed the television out of the changing rooms and carried it to his car to take home. As he got to the car and put it in his boot he turned around and the chairman was stood behind him and kindly asked Bails to put the tv back in to the changing room.

Gary said his goodbyes to us and that was that, the chairman released a few more players and had kept about 6 of us first team players but 2 were injured, the next game was against Blyth Spartans away at there ground. Our reserve coach Bully took charge for the game I had a slight knock but really I didn't want to play as I wasn't in the right frame of mind after that week. We got hammered as expected and if it was not for our goalkeeper John Kennedy it could have been double figures. During the next week Charlie had appointed Dave Bell as our manager, Dave had been a coach at Chester and was a good guy his training sessions were enjoyable and I played well in the few games he was in charge of. I'm not sure he knew what he was letting himself in for, he brought Neil Cossley in as his assistant. Neil was local in the area and had been managing at local level he knew his football too. We got off to a great start by earning a draw away to Redditch, our team was made up local players who were playing 8m leagues above there league they were playing in and 3 first team players. It was a great feeling after that game even though it was only a draw we expected to be hammered. That was as good as it got from then on in as we were getting thumped by four or 5 goals. I had managed to score 4 goals altogether in that period before I left and was playing some of the best football I had played for a while as I was relaxed playing. Everyone was putting bets on us at the bookies to get beat including some ex players and manager apparently. To be fair it was a sure bet until the bookmakers clocked on to it and stopped taking bets. A lot of people lost a few quid that day when we got a draw at Redditch though. A few weeks later I had a phone call from Charlie to say that he had been voted out by the shareholders and was sacked as chairman. I was shocked and wasn't sure what was going to happen now but had an idea that the club was going to go into liquidation. The bailiffs had come in and locked all of the doors, luckily my door was ok. Charlie was adamant he could fight against the decision legally but later found that he couldn't. Lynn also left the club after a long time At the dolly blue tavern. The only first team players left were Jimmy Kelly, Mark Quayle, Ubey and myself, myself and Jimmy were on contracts. The next day I had a call from the new owner Mick Hoyle, he told me the club was going into administration and the club couldn't afford my wage or Jimmy's so we could go for free or we would be released any way when the liquidates came in. The club had to get rid of all of there out goings and the team would now be on 30 pound a week each. The club were deducted 10 points and could even have to drop down 4 divisions at the end of the season which would be northwest counties division 2. I had to move out of the house in a month or pay the asking price of 450 pound a month plus bills. He said I could stay in the house until after Christmas.

Chapter 22

Up To Barrow

I DIDN'T WANT TO hang around if the club couldn't afford to pay me so I spoke to Phil at Barrow on the phone and went down to training with them on the Thursday. After negotiating a deal with Phil, which is no easy task I agreed a deal until the end of the season. I took a pay cut of £60 a week to what I was on at Lancaster but they gave me three lump sums which worked out better for me as it was a better wage over the season. Training was in Blackburn as only one of the squad players was from Barrow with the rest of the team from Liverpool mainly. I trained once and then played on the Saturday against Hucknall town at their ground in the FA trophy. I had a good debut in a 1-1 draw, the manager there was Kevin Wilson and assistant Garry Thompson who were at Kettering. We beat them in the replay on the Tuesday night to get us through to the next round. On Tuesday nights we trained at the JJB soccer dome in Blackburn and on Thursdays we trained on Astroturf. I knew a few lads up there already as Phil and his assistant Gary Bauress were at Lancaster and had taken a few ex players up there. I drove in with Liam and Stringy as there both from the same area, match days and at home the drive wasn't the best with there being no motorway and it was usually blowing a gale up at Barrow. With a slight slope on the pitch it was always an advantage if we kicked up the hill first half and then down in the second with the wind. There was a good set up at Barrow with a good squad but we weren't playing very good football with most of the games being scrappy. I was nominated for player of the month in the league for November. We played Farsley Celtic away in Leeds where we drew 2-2 and I got both goals although one of them did have a slight deflection, we had a team night out in Leeds after the game which was one of the best team nights I have been on. I was in good form and enjoying it at Barrow and then I got sent off against Worcester City in the next round of the Trophy. It was a stupid sending off after 20 minutes I had been fouled a couple of times and then when I was fouled again from behind I swung my arm out which caught the defender in the face. I received a 3-match ban, which would come in to affect after the Christmas period.

We played Lancaster City at home on Boxing Day, on the way to the game Becky's car broke down, one of the players Steve Skinner and his mum drove past and stopped to pick me up and take me to the game. We won 3-0 and I scored 1 after Ubey who was playing for Lancaster passed the ball to me and it put me through one on one with the goalkeeper whom I slid the ball under. On the Saturday we played Workington away where we drew 1-1. I managed to get on the scoresheet again after my strike partner Tom Pope who was on loan from Crewe nodded the ball down to me and I hit it first time into the corner with my left foot to score my 4th for Barrow and 8th of the season. We had played terribly in the first half but after a rollicking at half time we were by far the better team in the second half. We then played Lancaster away on new years day to round up the 3 games in the week, we won 2-0 in a tough game against a battling Lancaster side. That was my last game for a while as my suspension kicked in after the game, I went back home to Guernsey the next day to see my family as I didn't get a chance to get back for Christmas with all of the games.

We flew over in the morning and went to meet my dad for coffee in town in the afternoon at a café called dix nuef. He looked a bit rough when I saw him and I could tell he had been on a drinking session, after an hour or so and a milkshake Becky and me went to visit the rest of my family after arranging to meet dad again tomorrow. The next day I had a phone call from dad, don't worry son, I'm in the cells but I'm ok. I couldn't believe it, I had only been over a day and was looking forward to spending some time. He was in prison for not paying a fine of £2,400 that he had got from years ago. He only had to pay £10 a week off but he was messing about not paying it and giving them a pound sometimes instead of the ten to wind them up. It had caught up with him now and in Guernsey if you cant pay the fine with cash then you pay it off by serving the time equivalent to the fine, dads worked out at over 80 days. In one way I was relieved as he wasn't looking well with the drink but it was horrible every day knowing that he was behind bars. They say that if you ever have to do bird then the best place is Guernsey as it's a nice prison as far as prisons go. I said to him at least you'll get fit and healthy, I went to see him on the Thursday with Becky that was a strange experience and not a very nice one. We brought him a language book on Irish Gaelic. We wrote at least once a week and I was interested to hear what it was like inside as I had been reading a few prison books just before he went inside like Damage Done and Midnight Express but I'm sure it wouldn't be that bad in Guernsey. In the waiting room we had to show I.D and couldn't take anything in to give him, and along with all the other visitors we went into see him for the allocated 45 minutes. There was a red chair and 2 white chairs the red one being for the inmate and the guests to sit on the white ones. As we walked in dad sat down on the white one with out realising, as he hadn't got the glasses that we'd brought for him earlier in the day. 3 pairs he needed to wear at once unfortunately I have the same genes and also wear glasses god help me when I get older if they get as bad as his eyesight. Dad was in good spirits and had decided that he was going to do the time instead of getting a loan off of someone to pay it off. It was sad when the bell went and we had to go and leave him there but at least he knew a few people in there so hed be ok. In his letters he said it was ok in there during the week but he was really bored at the weekends but that was because he couldn't go to the pub, which I thought was a good thing. He could do lots of weight training and there was a pool table and table tennis where he said he was king of the wing at both. He had a t.v in his cell which he could have on as long as he wanted and he played in the prison football team on weekends on the Astroturf pitch it sounded alright to me but obviously it isn't and your freedom is taken from you. I felt for some of the other guys who I knew when I went to see dad who were on long sentences it must be hard although they had made mistakes.

I flew back to Manchester the next day after seeing dad, on the Saturday we were playing Reddich away, I was suspended for the game but had to travel. I was due to be at a wedding in Manchester and when the game was cancelled after driving half way down there I got a lift straight to Manchester. I just missed the wedding ceremony but had made it for the meal, a buffet in the Chinese restaurant all you can eat, and it was good. We had booked a weekend away to Rome on a city break, we flew there on the Sunday morning and came back on the Tuesday. We went to the Coliseum and the Vatican city amongst other sights which were beautiful and historic. Being a Roman Catholic the Vatican had been a place I had always wanted to visit and it was amazing. The Coliseum was great too where we hired a tour guide to take us round and described the many vicious battles that took place there amongst the gladiators and we couldn't wait to watch the film Gladiator again after that. When we got back I was straight to training from the airport. The Saturday after was the first of my suspension and it was nearly a month before I was available for selection. After coming on sub against Stalybridge for 15 minutes we were into February and I went on another city break to Prague, I wasn't missing any training or games, Prague was a lovely city although it was cold at the time we had a good weekend. Kettering Town at home was our next game and I was itching to play in this one, the team had been playing well though and I was sub but come on and done ok in the last 15 minutes. On the Saturday we played Worksop away where I got my first start for nearly 2 months, we played terribly and to make matters worse in the 80th minute I got my second booking and was sent off. My first booking was for a clumsy tackle and my second was for apparently swearing but in the referees report it had said that I just said bloody hell referee that wasn't a foul.

The next game I was on the bench as the manager wasn't happy with my sending off. I came on as sub when we were winning but then one of our players got sent off and Phil subbed me back off again, which is probably one of the most humiliating things that can happen to you as a footballer. I walked straight off towards the changing rooms before the lads were shouting me to come back to the dug out. I received another ban this time 2 games. When I was back in the team I started about 6 games but hadn't scored and was getting subbed even when I was playing well in the 4 games but the last 2 games I hadn't played well but played 90 minutes in both. I was dropped for a game but we had lost so I was starting for the next game against Harrogate away. I had got ill the night before the game and was up all night, I rang Phil first thing in the morning to let him know that I wasn't well. He thought I was telling lies and wanted me to travel to the game anyway, I could hardly get out of bed let alone travel 3 hours on a bus. I told him I couldn't so I didn't go to the game and after that game I was on the bench and frozen out which made me lose interest. We had a team night out in Barrow and ended up at the nightclub called The Boat, which is an old cruise boat turned into a nightclub on the harbour.

There was 2 games left in the season and we were safe from relegation, I played about 10 minutes altogether in the 2 games. I was now thinking that I didn't want to stay at Barrow and fancied a new challenge, after having a good start it was my fault with the sendings off I didn't play enough games. During the last couple of months of the season I had been in touch with Gary Williams who was playing out in Spain and was going to help me get fixed up with a team out there also. Gary was living only a few doors down from my mum's apartment in Gran Alicant with his family, my mum had spoken to him and asked where he was playing at. He emailed me to say that he was playing out there and if I wanted to come out he would help as much as he could. I had been studying Spanish for the past 2 years and I was really fancying the idea of playing out there and the fresh challenge. I had been playing in England non-league since I was 18 and was starting to get a bit bored of it, so I planned to go out there for pre-season.

On the last game of the season for Barrow we played Moor Green away and I stayed over at my sisters after the game as I had booked a holiday to India a day after the season had finished. I went out for 4 weeks with my mate Dan and Becky was coming out for over 2 weeks along with two other friends from Guernsey, Vanny and Dom. We met Dom in Delhi and he stayed with us for 3 days but didn't like the pollution and poverty so booked a flight back and cut short his 10-day visit. Whilst at Delhi airport meeting Dom, I bumped into my old team mate at Northwich Victoria who was now at Morecambe Chris Blackburn. He had just played in the play off final at Wembley where Morecambe had won promotion to the football league by beating Exeter City with Danny Carlton scoring the winner. I was pleased for them, as it was about time they had got promoted after coming close on a few occasions.

In India we flew to Delhi after having a night in Amsterdam as our flight was cancelled. When we got a taxi from the airport to the paraganj area there was cows and dogs on the roads and people asleep on the streets. I thought to myself I'm not going to like this but the next day when we woke up from our boiling hot room with no air con the streets were packed with life and shops, smells colours, noise it was amazing and nothing that I had seen before. After a few days in the hectic city we took an overnight bus trip to Manali in the mountains. It was a rocky journey up there and after a few days in the quiet and beautiful surroundings I had got food poisoning, I new id get it at some point. Ive never felt that ill in my life, I told Dan to find me a doctor and at first he thought I just had sunstroke. I told him there is no way that this is sunstroke I need a doctor now. The next minute Dan had said he seen a man appear out of the bushes with what looked to be a white medical bag of some sort. He didn't speak any English but had a needle with him, he took it out and came over to me, I said no way tablets will be fine keep that thing away from me. After a few hours Dan had to rush to the toilet and was violently ill I think he realised it wasn't sunstroke. We both felt a bit better after a couple of days but really we couldn't of been in a worse place to get ill, our room had no tv there was no food just water. The walls were bright blue and the place was packed with Israeli's who loved to play the Australian instrument. We were struggling to eat, as we didn't trust any of the restaurants that we had been to for they could have been the one that had given us food poisoning.

When we felt better we got a 10-hour bus trip across to Mcleod Ganj in Dharamasala the home of his holiness the Dalai Lama and many Tibetan refugees who escaped from Chinese rule in Tibet. Any of them had made the long walk across the Himalayas to India with some losing limbs from frostbite. We stayed in Mcleod Ganj for a couple of weeks and it was one of my favourite places, the first day we met a man from England called Mick who showed us around the place. I did a bead course learning how to make the traditional necklaces with gemstones and learning the meanings of the stones. Mcleod was a small town where you thought you were in Tibet with all the music food and shops most were Tibetans. We had another tough bus trip back down to Delhi to meet everyone from the airport. All 3 were coming in a day after each other, I booked myself into a better hotel as I couldn't stay in the one Dan booked us into. With no air con it smelt bad and was unbearably hot, Dan tried to stick it out and when I went to meet him he looked terrible and dehydrated so he booked a room in the same hotel that night. It was back at the paraganj area and the madness of the place there was some tourists and travellers there that have lost the plot completely. One guy balanced a glass ball on his head all day and there was European men and woman walking around barefoot with cows muck and bits of glass and dirt everywhere. It was about 5 pence for a pair of flip-flops. When everyone had arrived, we met Dom, Becky and then Vanny one by one from the airport and then took a taxi down to the Taj Mahal. Dom had been reading loads and telling us all about the Taj Mahal and how he was Anglo-Indian but didn't make the trip as he flew back that morning. After the beautiful Taj mahal we got another taxi up to Rishikesh the yoga capital of the world and stayed in Lacksman Jula. A place on the banks of the river Ganges it was a very holy place with lots of pilgrims and Sadhus. The place took a while getting used to and there was so many monkeys on the bridge you had to cross to get to the other side of the river. It was nice to be able to take a swim in the river though with the heat and humidity.

Before the trip at the airport in Birmingham I had a phone call from Phil, he said to me get fit over the summer and ring me when you get back. I never mentioned Spain as I thought just in case I decided not to go last minute, that was my back up plan until Ubey emailed me to say he had just read that I had been released. I just laughed to myself, why didn't Phil just tell me on the phone instead of doing it like that with out telling me. After India I was in England for 2 days before flying home to Guernsey, my nephews christening was on July 1st and Becky's mum and Nan were visiting Guernsey for the first time. I told them to come in June as the weather would be perfect but it wasn't, it rained the whole time they were there but they still managed to get over to Herm and have a ride on the horse and cart in Sark. I had managed to get a lot of training in Guernsey with my dad in the first few weeks we were up at 5am and jogging on the cliff paths. I was back in Guernsey for the longest amount of time for a while.

CHAPTER 23

VIVA ESPANA

IT WAS NICE TO spend time there seeing everyone, pre-season started a bit later in Spain than in England but not as late as I thought it did and when I got out there I found that they had been 3 or 4 weeks in to training. The plan was to fly back to England on the 10th of July and then get another flight to Alicante. My mum had suggested taking the smart car over to Spain that was a left handed drive. She had never got around to driving it over so I said I would. On the 25th of July Becky and I drove from St Malo after getting the ferry across from Guernsey our route took us through St Malo to Rennes, Nantes, Bordeaux, Toulouse, Perpignan, Barcelona, Valencia, Alicante and to Gran Alicant. It took us 3 days and we stayed over 2 nights in Avis hotels in Noirt and Perpignan. The Smart car was a lot better than I thought it would be and it was fine considering in Guernsey the speed limit is maximum 35mph.

When we arrived in at the apartment Gary was away on a course for 10 days. It was a holiday for the first 2 weeks but I got my jogs in the mornings in but needed to get some harder training with a team. We met up with Gary's agent called Vincente. He wasn't much help at all and the conversation was negative really. He was saying how hard it was if you couldn't communicate with the players, and how in the lower leagues in Spain it is so different to England the managers and clubs aren't very professional and wont really look at foreign players with no reputation in Spain.

After the drink we decided to go to Santa Pola to speak with the manager there at the preferente league club. The team was training and we were waiting for a chance to speak with the coach. When we managed to speak to the coach Gaz gave him his mobile phone so his friend on the other line could communicate for us. The coach said we needed to ask the president if we could train, we spoke with him through one of the Santa Pola players who translated for us. The president said that the team was a closed shop they had 25 players and we couldn't train. In the next few days we went around all of the local clubs around where we were and the answer was the same we couldn't train no trial closed shop of 25 players. It was becoming very frustrating and not at all how I imagined the clubs to be in Spain. The last hope was Javea but it was an hour and a half away but there were no other options so I rang the manager after getting his number from the clubs web site. The manager was English and I spoke with him on the phone and he sounded really keen for us to go up. Kenny Brown was the manager and he had said to come up any time on the Friday to train, as he would be at the club all day and we could have a chat with him before we trained. We drove up and got there early but there was no sign of Kenny, we waited for a couple of hours before all of the team had turned up so we just joined in with their training. The trainer was Spanish and he didn't speak any English, I had to follow what everyone else was doing in training and I really had to concentrate as the trainer was explaining the drills we were going to do. The first half-hour was really hard and I was worried I was going to look stupid but I started to enjoy it, I used the Spanish I did know to communicate with the rest of the lads and felt good after the 2 and a half-hour session. Javeas stadium was small with only 40 odd seats for the directors on one side of the ground and the main stand being steps where you could sit or stand on I think there average attendance was only 150-200 which is poor really compared to the crowds in England. They would be the equivalent to the smaller teams in the Unibond division one. Many of the teams in the Preferente and Tercera leagues are of similar set ups, with a lot of pitches being Astroturf.   Gary and myself had both trained well so we were both hopeful that the trainer would put a good word in for us to Kenny, it was annoying that he wasn't there though himself. After stopping off for a meal in Javea we worked out how much travelling would cost to travel up they're for training and matches 5 times a week. It was about 32 Euro a trip so that worked out 160 Euro per week between 2 of us. I figured we probably needed to be earning 1000 Euro at least for it to be worth while. I waited until Monday for Kenny to ring but when he didn't I called him up. He said to me that the coach was impressed with both of us and that he wanted us there but the problem would be wages. The average wage in the squad was 600 Euro a month, as he said that my phone cut off because the credit had run out. I put some credit on and called him back, he said you don't mess about do you. I told him that the money wasn't a problem at the moment and I would give it a go there for 600. Even though that was a terrible wage and id be coming out with hardly anything after petrol, but I wanted to give it a go so I said id except if Gaz did. I was surprised that he didn't want to see us again to have another look as he still hadn't seen us play and he hadn't even asked me what position I played in or where ive played at. Kenny had said he would speak to the president and see what his budget was but he would definitely ring me first thing in the morning to let me know one way or another. I went over to Gary's place to have a chat with him and I told him about the conversation I had with Kenny. It was strange because at first he was really keen and then at the end of the conversation I felt that he didn't want us. We agreed that if he offered us a deal we would accept it, we didn't have any other options and we could not see us getting another club if this fell through, we couldn't even get a training session. I said to him that if we don't get anything here then I was going back to England to play, it had been a month in Spain now and the season was nearly starting in England. I couldn't afford to hang about in Spain either, as I hadn't brought in any money for nearly 3 and a half months and I had only trained twice with football teams.

In the morning there was no phone call I hadn't slept very well thinking of the call and what I was going to do if he said no, it was now midday and no call I could sense what was going to happen now he just wont bother calling. I new he didn't want us but I wanted him to say it so I could get on with planning what I was going to do. I went over to see Gaz and he wasn't surprised he had this treatment from coaches for a year.

I hadn't realised how bad things were in the lower leagues of Spanish football. It seems that apart from La Liga and the Segunda leagues, the 3rd and 4th divisions that are regional didn't seem very professional and were poorly run. Apart from the odd team like Torreivieca who get a good support and are mainly all English, the crowds just aren't there like there is in the English lower leagues and I appreciate how good the English set up is now, all through the leagues. As far as I have seen and the stories Gary had told me there was definitely discrimination against us because we were English speaking it seemed a closed door at every club I went to as well as the clubs Gary had been to.

I didn't want to wait around in the house for the call so I went in to town with Becky shopping for my birthday present. I was really angry about what I had experienced at these clubs and it felt like I was 15 again going for trials and getting knocked back but this time I wasn't even getting a trial, it was hard to accept. Nick Mollet from the Guernsey press called me whilst I was shopping and he couldn't have caught at a better time as I was fuming waiting for this call off of Kenny and I told him straight what it had been like here. When I was coming out of a shopping centre I had a voicemail from Kenny who said that his budget was now full. His priority was to get a centre half in but if I had came earlier on he would of signed us or if I went back then he would sign us at a later date. I think if I went out to a foreign country to play again, which I would maybe do in the future. I would save a lot more money before going out because you don't know when you are going to get paid and I would try and get more contacts with a club before going out there. I'm not sure how genuine Kenny was because I never met him but I still couldn't understand why he didn't take a look at us himself especially with the squad he had wasn't very strong.

Chapter 24

LANCASTER CITY X3

I MADE THE DECISION to fly back to England a couple of days later on the Thursday and it wasn't a hard decision to make. Gaz dropped us both off at the airport and we got back in to Liverpool airport in the afternoon. I gave Ubey a text, he was still at Lancaster to see if I could go training that night. I thought ill train there for a while to get fit as it is local for me. I went down training and it felt good to be kicking a ball again and having a joke with the lads. After training the manager Barrie Stimson asked me to play for him on Saturday against Manchester United in his words. FC United of Manchester is their real name but they are a club who was formed when the Glaziers took over Man United. A lot of supporters boycotted Old Trafford and started their own club. They had won promotion 2 years on the bounce and were now in the same league as Lancaster the Unibond North division one. I said yes why not, he offered me a few quid, which I needed so I said id play. Barrie asked me to play 4 games, as he didn't want me to play Saturday and then leave after the game. I said I would as I could do with the match practise, this was going to be my pre-season as I had missed one for the first time in ten years.   Saturdays game was in front of 2,300 which is likely to be the biggest crowd ill play in front of all season. FC United are among the favourites to win that league so beating them 2-1 was a great start to the season and it was Lancaster's first win for months and there biggest home crowd for more than 50 years in a league game. I played 90 minutes and set the first goal up from a corner kick and was involved in the second. My legs were really heavy though and my fitness showed on the Tuesday night where we came crashing down to earth with a 3-0 hammering to Chorley at there ground. It was the worst game of football I have ever played in my life, my legs were that heavy I went to clear the ball away with my left foot and kicked the ground. I came off when we went 2-0 down and I rang my dad to say that's me done with football I'm finished. On Saturday we played Radcliffe Borough at their place I played as a striker and enjoyed the game a lot more than when I was on the left wing in the previous 2 games. We won 4-0 but the score line flattered us a bit. I had felt a bit fitter in the game but when I got back I was sick all night, I didn't feel well all weekend but we had a game against Mossley on the Monday and I played but came off at half time as I still felt rough. We lost 2-0 in a poor game, that was my fourth game but Barrie has asked me to play for him until I got another club. The Saturday after we played Radcliffe again this time in the FA Cup qualifier, at this level you near enough have to win the cup before going in to the first round proper. We got beat 3-0 and I sensed it was on the cards when I had a volley going straight in to the bottom corner cleared by one of my own players.

This is where I am at in my football, I'm still at Lancaster having played 5 games for them now and scoring no goals as yet. I have missed a pre season and although I have dropped down a couple of leagues I still haven't found it easy as it's a tough league and very physical with most teams having 7 or 8 players over 6 foot. I haven't scored since last January so before I look to move on to a higher league again I need to start scoring goals again and enjoy playing football again. I still want to play at as high a level as I can and I certainly haven't given up on my football yet. I had lost that burn in my belly that I had, it is slowly coming back to me with the more I play the game. I am now 26 years old and am looking forward to getting involved in coaching a bit more and getting something else as well as football as it is unlikely that I'm going to make a big living out of the game now. I have done my first coaching badge, which was easy. I am now going to do my level 2 coaching badge, which starts in November. I had gained experience from coaching in Ireland as well as doing some coaching at Morecambe where I am still doing some coaching in schools. I am planning to go out to Australia when my girlfriend finishes her degree in 2 years to play. I have enjoyed playing football all of my life. I set out from Guernsey to make a living out of playing and ive done that, I got capped at under 18 and 21 level for Northern Ireland which I never thought I would. The game has taken me to some great places and stadiums and ive met lots of good people along the way. Ive exceeded my expectations when I first came over to England 9 years ago and stayed at my mate Scott's house. Where we looked for a team to play for and the better I did the more I expected from myself but I made some bad decisions along the way and I think that little bit of luck or decision making I didn't quiet get right. But I don't regret anything because there isn't any point. There is no other job in the world that I would rather do then to play football and I am fortunate to be able to make a living from the game. I have taken that for granted in the last year and I now have to work hard again to get back playing to the standard I was at. Making the move from Guernsey to England to improve my football and follow my dream at 17 was the best thing I have ever done.

CHAPTER 25

<u>GUERNSEY FOOTBALL</u>

IN MY OPINION THE way to improve Channel Island football is Guernsey to join forces with Jersey to help each other move forward. Now is the time to think how the channel island football can get on a bigger scale. From what I can gather the other team sports rugby and cricket is miles ahead and are moving with times and the need to fulfil the interests of their players. Unless this road has been explored and there is no chance of going down this road which to my knowledge, hasn't been publicised. I cant see why the channel islands cant take part in the world cup qualifiers, European championship qualifiers etc. Surely that would be the biggest inspiration any player would have to want to play football and it would improve the local game no end. Not to mention the support it would generate and of course income. It would get people into the ground to watch the island team in these big games and it would spiral down into the local league where fans would watch their favourite team. Money would probably be a major factor obviously but the Channel Islands are a rich place and some of the countries that enter the national tournaments all over the world are below the poverty line. Surely that couldn't be an excuse and I would hope that it wouldn't be the pride thing Guernsey and Jersey have to be a barrier between improvements of the game.

The other avenue to go down is inviting teams over like the past and selling the island to professional football clubs in the way of advertising how great Guernsey would be to have a week or so of pre-season training. Jersey has had some excellent tournaments in the last couple of years but I don't think Guernsey entered. The cliff paths must be some of best training you can get and managers would love putting their players through their paces up and down Jerbourg steps. Supporters and football lovers would be intrigued to see how pro clubs go about there business in pre-season training and the different methods, there could even be a few clubs here at a time with mini tournaments. A lot of clubs would probably pay there own way as a lot of teams go somewhere for a week in pre-season for team bonding and fitness regimes away from the club, why not Guernsey be the place for your summer training? Plenty of pitches to train and the beach training is also popular with professional teams. There seems to be improvement in the minis set ups with more coaches wanting to improve and taking there coaching badges and full credit to them for going out of there way to help and coach kids for no financial gain. I think it is brilliant the amount of time and effort that goes into minis football and also not forgetting the senior football which is also time consuming and takes a lot of effort sometimes it can be harder in adult football as you've then got to motivate players as with kids they just want to play. I think the south west counties are a good idea but at the same time it was costing players a lot of money and time off work it didn't seem to work out the way people would have wanted although it was a step up in standard. It would be better in my opinion to enter some bigger tournaments like the non-league home internationals with Wales Ireland England Holland and Italy representative teams play each other. Of course the standard would be extremely high with quality players but is that not the point of it. Again I'm sure fans here would love to go down and watch some entertaining football with quality players on show even if the channel island team or Guernsey were on the other end of some bad results I am sure those results would get better as time went on. The Murratti is the biggest game of the year and is a tradition that should be kept but there is no reason why that should be the only game. Again some people would say money is an issue but with what these games could possibly attract and how it could be advertised with papers, channel tv, videos of the games memorabilia, programmes attendances, sponsorship etc. I have been away from Guernsey football for a while so I don't know all of the facts the above is simply some ideas which may or may not have been explored.

Printed in the United Kingdom
by Lightning Source UK Ltd.
130263UK00002B/103-207/P